RECORD OF THE

5TH (SERVICE) BATTALION

THE

CONNAUGHT RANGERS

FROM

19TH AUGUST, 1914, TO 17TH JANUARY, 1916

PREFATORY NOTE

THE following short record of the services of the
5th (Service) Battalion of the Rangers has been
prepared, from the date the Battalion was raised
on 19th August, 1914, to the time of the arrival
of the Battalion in Rendina Bay, Greece, in order
that the brave and gallant deeds and the loyal
and persevering efforts of all ranks of the regiment may not be lost to history.

May, 1916.

MAPS

I

RECORD OF THE 5TH (SERVICE) BATTALION THE CONNAUGHT RANGERS

FROM 19TH AUGUST, 1914, TO 30TH JUNE, 1915.

ON the outbreak of hostilities, recruiting for the Connaught Rangers was opened at Galway on the 6th August, 1914, under War Office authority received by wire.

On the 9th August, 1914, Captain M. H. C. de C. Wickham, Lieuts. H. B. W. Maling and G. J. B. E. Massy arrived from Aldershot with 15 N.C.O.s, of whom 4 were sergeants and 11 corporals, to act as drill instructors to the new Battalion. Recruiting at first was only fair, but afterwards went on exceedingly well.

Major H. F. N. Jourdain proceeded from Crosshaven to Galway on the 11th August and took over charge of the recruiting in the 88th Recruiting Area.

On the 19th August, 1914, Major H. F. N. Jourdain was appointed to the command of the 5th (Service) Battalion the Connaught Rangers, as the new Battalion now became, and was granted the temporary rank of Lieut.-Colonel from that date.

On the 22nd August, 1914, Lieut.-Colonel Jourdain proceeded to Dublin, and there took over command of 220 N.C.O.s and men, who left

Galway on that date for Dublin under Captain Wickham and Lieut. Maling. This party arrived at Richmond Barracks, Dublin, at 3.30 p.m. on the 22nd August, and Lieut. Maling assumed the duties of Adjutant from the same date.

Captain G. F. Callaghan, 1st Battalion, joined also on the 22nd August, but was sent to the 1st Battalion on the 29th August.

Captain N. C. K. Money, 22nd Punjabis, joined on the 24th August for attachment, and Lieut. and Quartermaster P. Farrell was taken on the strength from the same date, and was promoted Quartermaster from the 25th August.

Lieut.-General Sir Bryan T. Mahon, K.C.V.O., C.B., D.S.O., assumed command of the 10th (Irish) Division on the 24th August, and visited Richmond Barracks on the same date to see the men of the Battalion who had already joined.

On the 27th August, Colonel (retired) R. J. Cooper, C.V.O., who had been appointed Brigadier-General to command the 29th Brigade, in which the Battalion was included, visited the barracks, and saw the men of the Battalion.

A draft of 109 N.C.O.s and men, under Lieut. S. H. Lewis of the Connaught Rangers, arrived in Dublin and joined on the 28th August.

The 5th (Service) Battalion was now included in the 29th Infantry Brigade with the 5th Royal Irish Regiment, the 6th Royal Irish Rifles, and the 6th Leinster Regiment.

Captain A. S. Hog, Reserve of Officers, late of the Connaught Rangers, joined the Battalion on the 29th August, 1914.

Major G. C. Digan, Reserve of Officers, late of
the Connaught Rangers, joined the Battalion on
the 31st August.

Two N.C.O.s and 107 men joined the Battalion
on the 31st August on posting from the dépôt,
under command of Captain H. J. Nolan-Ferrall,
who returned to Galway on completion of the duty.

A draft composed of 67 N.C.O.s and men
arrived at Richmond Barracks, Dublin, on the
2nd September, 1914.

A draft of 57 N.C.O.s and men arrived from
the dépôt on the 4th September, being posted
mostly to B and C Companies.

On the 5th September a further draft of 50
N.C.O.s and men arrived in Dublin, and were
also posted to B and C Companies.

Captain H. J. Nolan-Ferrall joined the Battalion
on the 4th September.

Lieut. J. H. N. H. Burke, Reserve of Officers,
reported himself for duty on the 7th September.

Lieut. G. J. B. E. Massy, the Connaught
Rangers, and 94 N.C.O.s and men joined the
Battalion on the 7th September.

A draft of 25 N.C.O.s and men joined the
Battalion, still at Richmond Barracks, on the
8th September.

The nucleus of four Companies had now been
formed, and the strength of the Battalion was
now over 650 N.C.O.s and men, with 8 officers,
not including the Commanding Officer, Adjutant,
and Quartermaster.

The Battalion left Richmond Barracks, Dublin,
on the 10th September, at 7 a.m., and proceeded

to Fermoy *en route* for Kilworth Camp. Strength, 10 officers and 629 men. Fermoy was reached at 1.50 p.m., and the Battalion marched to Kilworth Camp, which was reached at 4.35 p.m. Here the Battalion occupied huts, while some of the men were put under canvas. A small party had been left in Dublin to hand over barracks.

Captain A. L. Keogh, Reserve of Officers, late of the Connaught Rangers, joined the Battalion on the 10th September.

A draft composed of 137 N.C.O.s and men joined the Battalion at Kilworth Camp on 11th September.

A draft composed of 47 N.C.O.s and men joined the Battalion at Kilworth also on the 11th September.

Lieut. H. B. W. Maling's appointment as Adjutant was confirmed in the *London Gazette* and dated 22nd August.

Late in the evening of the 11th September, 350 recruits from Pontefract, England, joined the Battalion at Kilworth Camp. They were mostly composed of men who had been enlisted in Yorkshire for the York and Lancaster Regiment.

2nd Lieut. Richard Ross Martin joined the Battalion as 2nd Lieutenant on the 13th September, having been gazetted to the Battalion from the Officers' Training Corps, Dublin.

Lieut. and Quartermaster I. P. Praeger, 6th (Service) Battalion, which was about to be formed, joined the 5th Battalion on the 13th September, in accordance with War Office instructions.

On the 14th September a draft composed of

51 N.C.O.s and men joined the Battalion at 1914 Kilworth Camp from the dépôt.

Twelve men joined the Battalion from Dublin on the 15th September.

Major G. C. Digan proceeded to Galway on the 16th September for duty at the dépôt.

Captain B. R. Cooper, late 2nd Lieutenant Royal Field Artillery and Captain Special Reserve, Royal Field Artillery, joined the Battalion at Kilworth Camp on the 16th September, on appointment to the Battalion.

On the 17th September a draft of 70 N.C.O.s and men joined the Battalion at Kilworth Camp from the dépôt.

Four clerks of the A.S.C. Staff Clerks' section joined the Battalion on the 17th September from Aldershot. They were lent as a temporary measure to the Battalion.

The following drafts joined the Battalion :—

On 18th September, 38 N.C.O.s and men joined from Galway.

On 18th September, 5 men joined from Glasgow.

On 21st September, 15 N.C.O.s and men joined from Galway.

Major C. T. W. Forth, late Indian Army, joined on the 18th September.

Major A. W. H. Bell, late the Connaught Rangers, joined on the 17th September.

2nd Lieut. A. St. J. Mahony joined on the 21st September.

A Company, 6th Battalion, was formed on the 21st September, and 260 N.C.O.s and men were transferred to that unit by order of the War Office.

2nd Lieut. G. B. Lee joined on the 23rd September.

2nd Lieut. B. W. Bond joined on the 24th September.

Major C. W. Bowlly, Reserve of Officers, joined the Battalion for attachment to the 6th Battalion on the 24th September.

The following drafts joined the Battalion :—

Nineteen N.C.O.s and men on the 23rd September from Galway.

Twenty-two N.C.O.s and men on the 24th September from Galway.

Both these drafts joined A Company, 6th Battalion.

Captain A. L. Keogh was admitted to Hospital on the 24th September, and was invalided on the 26th September.

2nd Lieut. M. J. Fogarty joined the Battalion on the 24th September.

2nd Lieut. G. Mortimer joined the Battalion on the 26th September.

2nd Lieut. O. M. Tweedy joined the Battalion on the 26th September.

2nd Lieut. J. W. Cartmel-Robinson joined the Battalion on the 27th September.

2nd Lieut. T. S. P. Martin joined the Battalion on the 26th September.

2nd Lieut. A. T. A. Nesbitt joined the Battalion on the 28th September.

2nd Lieut. A. J. Kearney joined the Battalion on the 28th September.

2nd Lieut. D. P. J. Kelly joined the Battalion on the 30th September.

All drafts joining the Battalion were posted to the 6th Battalion, which was attached and was now commanded by Major C. W. Bowlly, in readiness for a sudden move.

The details 6th Battalion, strength 3 officers, 1 Quartermaster, and 340 other ranks under Major C. W. Bowlly, left Kilworth Camp for Moore Park, Fermoy, there to be stationed.

Captain Sir Andrew Armstrong, Bart., joined the Battalion on appointment on the 28th September.

2nd Lieut. E. O'Connor joined on the 1st October.

By 10th Division Order No. 27 (3) dated 3rd October, 2nd Lieuts. A. T. A. Nesbitt, G. Haire, and P. W. Bain were transferred to the 6th Battalion, then at Moore Park.

2nd Lieut. Bain reported his arrival on the 4th October, but proceeded to Moore Park.

2nd Lieuts. de C. O'Grady and F. J. Charlton joined on the 5th October.

The Battalion being under orders to move to Dublin, an advance party under Lieut. Massy and 40 N.C.O.'s and men left Kilworth on the 5th October for Royal Barracks to take over quarters.

The Battalion left Kilworth Camp on the 9th October by march route, and entrained at Fermoy in two trains leaving at 10 a.m. and 10.15 a.m. the same date.

A and B Companies left by the first train with Headquarters, and C and D under Major Bell in the second train.

The Battalion arrived in Dublin at 2.15 p.m.

and 3 p.m., and took over quarters in the Royal Barracks, in Arbour Hill and Horse Square.

Lieut.-General Sir B. T. Mahon visited the barracks on the 10th October and inspected the Battalion.

Major-General Vesey J. Dawson, C.V.O., Inspector of Infantry for Ireland, inspected the Battalion in marching order at 11 a.m. on the 14th October, and complimented the Battalion on the fine physique of the men, and their general turn-out.

In the afternoon the Battalion was also inspected at field operations in the Phoenix Park.

Captain A. Webber joined the Battalion on the 15th October. He had formerly belonged to the 3rd Battalion of the Rangers, and had served in South Africa with the 1st Battalion and the Mounted Infantry.

Captain M. H. C. Wickham left the Battalion on the 19th October, to the great regret of all ranks, to join the 2nd Battalion the Royal Irish Regiment, then operating with the Expeditionary Force.

Drill-Sergt. John Hudson, from the Irish Guards, joined the Battalion as Sergt.-Major on the 19th October.

Sergt.-Major Hudson formerly served with the Connaught Rangers and Irish Guards.

Captain F. C. Burke, from District Inspector R.I.C., joined the Battalion as Captain on the 27th October.

A Company commenced musketry at Dollymount on the 4th November.

25 recruits joined the Battalion from Galway on the 7th November.

1 recruit joined the Battalion from Castlebar on 1914 the 7th November.

32 recruits joined the Battalion from Galway on the 9th November.

The strength of the Battalion on the 6th November, 1914, was :—

> 29 officers.
> 1 warrant officer.
> 83 N.C.O.s.
> 485 trained men.
> 519 recruits.
> Total, all ranks, 1,117.

Forty-four batmen and servants were also attached to the Battalion. These numbers do not include the two drafts mentioned above.

Major A. W. H. Bell was appointed second in command of the Battalion, dated 9th November.

The following officers joined the Battalion at Dublin on the dates mentioned :—

2nd Lieut. H. T. Godber on the 16th November.
2nd Lieut. A. C. Holmes on the 16th November.
2nd Lieut. R. J. H. Shaw on the 16th November.
2nd Lieut. T. W. G. Johnson on the 18th November.
2nd Lieut. E. J. G. Kelly on the 18th November.
2nd Lieut. O. H. Acton on the 18th November.

2nd Lieut. de C. O'Grady, 1 company sergt.-major, 1 corporal, and 12 privates left the Battalion on the 28th November for the Curragh as advance party for the Divisional Cyclist Company.

7 recruits joined from Galway and Castlebar on the 16th November.

60 recruits joined from Galway on the 27th November.

1 recruit joined from Galway on the 21st November.

1 recruit joined from Castlebar on the 21st November.

2nd Lieut. J. E. Burke joined on the 30th November.

Two lance-corporals and 15 privates proceeded to the Curragh on the 1st December, and were transferred to the Divisional Cyclist Company there stationed.

2nd Lieut. A. D. Mulligan joined on the 7th December.

Lieut. A. J. W. Blake joined on the 8th December.

A Company proceeded on a company march on the 8th December, to Dunboyne, Leixlip, and thence back to Dublin on the 10th December.

The Establishment of the 5th (Service) Battalion was increased by 50 rank and file by War Office Letter dated 2nd December 1914.

Total for all ranks 1,157.

Commanding Officers were empowered to make arrangements with O.C. Dépôts to make up the deficiency at once.

2nd Lieut. C. F. B. Harvey joined on the 10th December.

Lieut. and Adjutant H. B. W. Maling was promoted temporary Captain from the 18th November 1914.

2nd Lieut. E. O'Connor was promoted Lieutenant on 18th November.

Captain H. J. Nolan-Ferrall was promoted Temp.-Major from 19th November.

2nd Lieuts. B. W. Bond and R. R. Martin were promoted Temp.-Lieutenants from the 19th November.

. 2nd Lieut. T. A. Kean joined on the 21st December. 17 recruits from the dépôt joined the same day.

B Company proceeded on a company march on the 10th December, and returned to Headquarters on the 11th December, on account of inclement weather.

All men of the Battalion who had not been guilty of misbehaviour were granted free warrants to their homes for seven days to those who lived in England, and for six days to those domiciled in Ireland, as a special concession during the Christmas leave period. Training, however, went on as usual for those who remained.

Major C. T. W. Forth proceeded on the 29th December to Salisbury to take up the position of R.T.O., and was struck off the strength accordingly.

Major-General V. J. Dawson, C.V.O., Inspector of Infantry for Ireland, inspected the Battalion at field operations near Rathfarnham on the 30th December, 1914.

Lieut. H. T. Hewitt, 1st Battalion, was attached to the Battalion from the 4th January, 1915.

2nd Lieut. H. J. Shanley joined on the 5th January, 1915.

Captain Sir A. Armstrong, Bart., proceeded to Galway on the 7th January, 1915, for duty at the dépôt.

1915   2nd Lieut. H. H. L. Richards joined on the (
January.

Lieut. V. J. Tibbs joined on the 9th January

2nd Lieut. G. R. Bennett joined on the 1ᵢ
January.

Captain N. C. K. Money was promoted to 1
temporary rank of Major in the 5th Battalion, a
Lieut. G. J. B. E. Massy was promoted to the te
porary rank of Captain, dated 28th December, 19

The strength of the Battalion on the 9th Janua
1915, was :—

41 officers.
1 warrant officer.
96 sergeants and corporals.
800 trained men.
173 recruits.

Total, all ranks, 1,111.

There were besides 52 specially enlisted batm
and 3 attached men.

All companies except the latest recruits h
completed musketry before the close of the ye

2nd Lieut. D. J. Cowan joined on the 1ᵢ
January.

2nd Lieut. T. A. Kean left the Battalion
the 20th January, pending resignation.

The Battalion commenced 'battalion trainir
on the 18th January in Dublin, and 'brigade tra
ing' was brought into force on the 25th Januai

On the 1st February, 1915, an advance party
3 officers and 100 rank and file left by train for 1
Curragh Camp, to take over quarters at Beresfᵢ
Barracks, Curragh Camp.

The headquarters and the Battalion left Dublin 1915 by march route on the 2nd February, for Naas, *en route* for the Curragh Camp, with the 6th Royal Irish Rifles, at 8 a.m., and after a tiring march in very heavy rain and a high wind reached Naas at 2 p.m. the same date.   The Battalion was billeted in the town, mostly in the Town Hall, the Gaol, and in some old stables in the town.

On the 3rd February, the Battalion marched independently to the Curragh, starting at 9.30 a.m., and reached Beresford Barracks soon after 12.30 p.m., where it took over quarters.

The 6th Royal Irish Rifles arrived at the Curragh on the 3rd February, and the 6th Leinster Regt. reached camp on the 2nd February by train, from Birr.

Lieut. J. H. N. H. Burke, after appearing before a Medical Board, was granted 3 months' sick leave, and left the Battalion, being struck off the strength in consequence.

The following drafts arrived from the dépôt at Galway :—

On the 12th February 13 men joined.
On the 15th February 50 men joined.
On the 19th February 39 men joined.
On the 24th February 22 men joined.

After arrival at the Curragh, the Battalion was ordered to perform 2 days a week brigade training, 1 day battalion training, 2 days individual and platoon training, and 1 day company training.

Four sergeants and 1 corporal who had been attested for home service, and who would not proceed with the Battalion, were posted to the

B

3rd Battalion at Kinsale, and proceeded there on the 1st March.

Lieut. H. T. Hewitt, 1st Battalion, who had been attached to the 5th Battalion, left on the 4th March to rejoin his Battalion.

On the 15th March, Q.M.-Sergt. Brook and 102 N.C.O.s and men proceeded to join the 3rd Battalion at Kinsale, as medically unfit for service abroad.

The following officers were promoted as stated against their names :—

Temp.-Lieut. B. W. Bond to Temp.-Captain, from 7th January.

Temp.-2nd Lieut. G. B. Lee to Temp.-Lieut., from 28th January.

Temp.-2nd Lieut. O. M. Tweedy to Temp.-Lieut., from 29th January.

Temp.-2nd Lieut. F. J. Charlton to Temp.-Lieut., from 30th January.

Temp.-2nd Lieut. T. S. P. Martin to Temp.-Lieut., from 31st January.

Temp.-2nd Lieut. J. W. Cartmel-Robinson to Temp.-Lieut., from 1st February.

Temp.-2nd Lieut. R. J. H. Shaw to Temp.-Lieut., from 9th February.

Eleven N.C.O.s and men proceeded to join the 3rd Battalion at Kinsale on the 23rd March. Four of these N.C.O.s were sent to relieve the two sergeants and two corporals, from the Expeditionary Force, who arrived from the details at Kinsale to be attached to the Battalion for instruction. They had been sent home for wounds or sickness and had formerly belonged to the 1st or 2nd

Battalions, and were now attached to the 5th Battalion for instructional purposes.

The Battalion was issued with the 1914 equipment and the short rifle on the 18th, 19th, and 20th of March. The web equipment and long rifles were taken in and returned to store.

In the *London Gazette* of the 24th March, 1915, Lieut. E. O'Connor relinquished his commission on account of ill health, dated the 25th March.

Major A. W. H. Bell left the Battalion on the 29th March, having appeared before a Medical Board on the 23rd.

Lieut. J. I. O'Sullivan, R.A.M.C., joined the Battalion as Medical Officer on the 21st March.

2nd Lieut. G. Robinson joined on the 27th March.

By a War Office Letter dated 12th March, it was intimated that Temp.-2nd Lieutenants in excess of war establishment will, on a Battalion proceeding abroad, be retained at home, and attached to a Reserve Battalion of the unit, with a view to filling vacancies caused by casualties at the front. It is, therefore, in the interests of all Battalions to train as large a reserve of 2nd Lieutenants as possible.

By the same order, commanding officers were empowered to select the most proficient to complete the numbers up to establishment, irrespective of date of appointment, on a Battalion being ordered to proceed on service.

All recruits and men unfit for service abroad, who could not be made efficient, were ordered to be sent to Kinsale to join the 3rd Reserve Battalion.

2nd Lieut. John Wallace joined the Battalion on the 29th March.

2nd Lieut. P. J. McGlade joined on the 1st April.

The Battalion was inspected by Brigadier-General R. J. Cooper, C.V.O., commanding 29th Brigade, on the 6th April, at Beresford Barracks, Curragh Camp, who expressed himself as well pleased with the appearance of the Battalion, and informed the parade that the Lieutenant-General commanding the 10th Division was very pleased with the way the whole Battalion moved and was handled on field operations.

The Battalion paraded on the 16th April with the 29th Brigade, and all units of the 10th Division, except the 31st Brigade and the 7th Royal Dublin Fusiliers at Dublin, and the Signal Company at Carlow, for inspection by the General Officer commanding the 10th Division (Lieut.-General Sir B. T. Mahon, K.C.V.O., C.B., D.S.O.). After forming up in line of mass, the Battalion marched past in mass, and again forming up in line of mass, advanced in review order. The Rangers paraded for the inspection at 10 a.m., but did not return to Barracks until 1.35 p.m. The turn-out and drill of the whole Battalion was excellent, and the march past could not have been better.

Major Bell was transferred to the 9th Battalion King's Own Shropshire Light Infantry by Irish command order, dated 17th April, and was ordered to join that unit on the termination of his medical leave.

The Rangers were now warned to be ready to

move to a point of concentration near Aldershot,
about the end of April.

On the 25th April, an advance party of 1 officer
(Lieut. Blake) and 20 N.C.O.s and men left for
Basingstoke to take over camp.

The train transport and second line were ordered
to proceed by march route to Dublin, and thence
to embark for Liverpool *en route* for Basingstoke.

The Battalion was ordered to be ready to move
to Basingstoke about the 2nd May.

The following officers were selected to proceed
to England to the place of concentration :—

Lieut.-Colonel H. F. N. Jourdain (Commanding).

Major H. J. Nolan-Ferrall.

Major N. C. K. Money.

Captain A. S. Hog.

Captain B. R. Cooper.

Captain A. Webber.

Captain F. C. Burke.

Captain G. J. B. E. Massy.

Captain B. W. Bond.

Lieut. S. H. Lewis (Machine-gun Officer).

Lieut. R. R. Martin (Assist. M.G.O.).

Lieut. A. J. W. Blake.

Lieut. O. M. Tweedy.

Lieut. F. J. Charlton.

Lieut. T. S. P. Martin.

Lieut. R. J. H. Shaw (Scout Officer).

2nd Lieut. G. Mortimer.

2nd Lieut. M. J. Fogarty (Transport Officer).

2nd Lieut. E. J. G. Kelly.

2nd Lieut. H. T. Godber (Signal Officer)

2nd Lieut. J. E. Burke.

2nd Lieut. A. C. Holmes.

2nd Lieut. A. D. Mulligan.

2nd Lieut. T. W. G. Johnson.

2nd Lieut. G. R. Bennett.

2nd Lieut. G. F. B. Harvey.

2nd Lieut. J. Wallace.

Captain and Adjutant H. B. W. Maling.

Lieut. and Quartermaster P. Farrell.

Sergt.-Major J. Hudson.

Lieut. J. W. Cartmel-Robinson and 2nd Lieut. A. St. J. Mahony, with Lieut. Tibbs, 2nd Lieuts. H. H. L. Richards and H. J. Shanley, were left behind on the sick list.

The following officers proceeded to Kinsale on the 29th April to be attached to the 3rd Battalion:—

Lieut. G. B. Lee.

2nd Lieut. O. H. Acton.

2nd Lieut. A. J. Kearney.

2nd Lieut. G. Robinson.

2nd Lieut. P. J. McGlade,

and five Batmen.

2nd Lieut. D. P. J. Kelly was left behind to give over barracks and to be in charge of details. He later rejoined the Battalion at Basingstoke.

The 10th Division commenced to embark for England on the 26th April, the advance parties proceeding on that date.

The 5th Battalion left the Curragh Camp on the 4th May for Dublin by two trains from the Curragh siding at 3 p.m. and 3.15 p.m., and thence by rail, reached the North Wall, Dublin, at 4.20 p.m., and almost immediately embarked on board the hired transport   , one of the

Harwich and Hook of Holland liners. Major-
General Friend, C.B., commanding the Forces in
Ireland, was present at the docks, and came to
wish the Battalion farewell, and to say how
gratified he was with the Battalion.

Colonel M. G. Moore, C.B., who commanded
the 1st Battalion, 1902–6, was present to wish the
Battalion 'God speed', while presents of cigarettes,
pipes, chocolate, and matches, were generously
distributed to the men by a committee of Irish
ladies.

The naval and military embarkation officers
both at North Wall and Holyhead complimented
the Commanding Officer on the good behaviour
and orderliness of the N.C.O.s and men of the
Battalion, which had made the embarkation at
Dublin and the disembarkation at Holyhead so
easy.   The crossing to Holyhead passed without
incident, although a hostile submarine had been
seen at Holyhead on the afternoon of the 4th May.

One Company, 6th Leinster Regiment, under
Captain D'Arcy Irvine, crossed with the Battalion
in H.M. Transport   . Curiously enough, this
same Company also proceeded from Mudros to the
Peninsula in the   in the August following.

The troops were delayed three hours at Holyhead to enable the mail to proceed in front, and
the first train arrived at Basingstoke at 10.20 a.m.
on the 5th May, when the first half Battalion
detrained at once and marched to New Park
Camp, Hackwood, which was reached at 11.30 a.m.
The 6th Royal Irish Rifles and the 10th Hants
were already in camp there.   The left half Battalion

arrived soon afterwards, and reached camp at midday on the 5th May.

On the 6th May the Battalion was ordered suddenly to fall in for inspection by General Sir A. Hunter, G.C.B., G.C.V.O., D.S.O. ; but after a short inspection the men were dismissed.

On the 7th May the Battalion took part in a Brigade route march, the weather being very hot and sultry.

The Battalion transport and heavy baggage arrived from Liverpool on the 6th May at 5.30 a.m. The Battalion was exercised daily in Brigade.

On the 12th May the Battalion marched in Brigade from New Park at 9.45 a.m., and with the remainder of the 10th Division took part in a march, and billeted at night at Greywell. Outposts were mounted, and at 6.30 a.m. on the 13th May the Brigade resumed its march in pouring rain, which interfered much with the operations. At 2.20 p.m. the Brigade began to march to camp in torrential rain from Long Sutton, reaching camp at 4.30 p.m. the same date.

The Battalion operated from Basingstoke until the 19th May. The Machine-gun detachment, under Lieuts. S. H. Lewis and R. R. Martin, proceeded to Bordon Camp on the 16th May for practice.

2nd Lieut. D. P. J. Kelly rejoined the Battalion from the Curragh on the 14th May, having completed the handing over of barracks at that station.

2nd Lieut. A. St. J. Mahony rejoined the Battalion on the 22nd May at Aldershot.

The Battalion marched through Odiham on the 19th May, and went into billets at Great Rye Farm on the same night. The following day the Battalion, with the 29th Brigade, took part in operations with the 12th Division of the Aldershot Command, on the conclusion of which the Battalion returned to billets at Great Rye Farm.

On the 21st May the Battalion marched in Brigade to Rushmoor Camp, Aldershot, and took over the camp left vacant by the 41st Brigade, which had proceeded to the Expeditionary Force. The Battalion went through a short course of musketry on the Ash Ranges on the 22nd May, remained at Aldershot on the 23rd May, and returned to Basingstoke on the 24th, halting at Hook Common at midday for dinners, and reaching camp at 4.30 p.m. without any men having fallen out. General Sir A. Hunter inspected the Brigade on the march near Hook Common. On the 25th May the Battalion took part in night operations from 6 p.m. that day until 2.20 a.m. the 26th.

The 10th Division had a rehearsal for the parade before His Majesty The King on the 27th. On the 28th May the Battalion paraded at 8 a.m. and marched in Brigade to Hackwood Park, where the whole of the 10th Division, less the 31st Brigade, were assembled. His Majesty The King arrived a few minutes past 11 a.m., and, after being received with a royal salute, rode down the line and inspected each Corps. The Infantry then marched past first, followed by the Royal Field Artillery and the Heavy Brigade, and the squadron of South Irish Horse.

The Battalion returned to camp at 12.50 p.m. and paraded again for night operations at 4.45 p.m. in the neighbourhood of Hackwood.

On the 1st June the whole of the 10th Division paraded at 9.15 a.m. for inspection by the Secretary of State for War (Field-Marshal Earl Kitchener, K.G., &c.), the parade being formed up at 12 o'clock.

After the general salute the Field-Marshal rode down the lines, and the troops then marched past.

The following complimentary orders were afterwards issued :—

10th Division Order No. 34, dated 1st June, 1915. Inspection by H.M. The King on 28th May, 1915.

' Lieut.-General Sir B. T. Mahon has received His Majesty's command to publish a Divisional Order to say how pleased His Majesty was to have had an opportunity of seeing the 10th Irish Division, and how impressed he was in the general appearance and physical fitness of the troops. H.M. The King recognizes that it is due to the keenness and co-operation of all ranks that the 10th Division has reached such a high standard of efficiency.'

Inspection by the Secretary of State for War on the 1st June.

Divisional Order No. 34. Dated 1st June, 1915.

' The G.O.C. 10th Irish Division has much pleasure in conveying to the troops that Field-Marshal Earl Kitchener of Khartoum, the Secretary of State for War, expressed himself as highly satisfied with all he saw of the 10th Division at the inspection to-day.'

On the 2nd June the Battalion marched in Brigade to Thatcham, and went into billets on that night, afterwards taking part in operations near Kingsclere and Newbury, returning to camp at Basingstoke at 3 p.m. on the 4th June, having bivouacked near Cannon Heath Farm on the previous night.

During these three days' operations and marching not a single man of the Battalion fell out, although the weather was very hot on the 2nd and 4th June.

The Brig.-General highly complimented all ranks of the Battalion on their excellent performance.

The Battalion proceeded with the remainder of the 10th Division to the neighbourhood of Strathfieldsaye and Aldermaston for operations, bivouacking from the 9th to 11th June, and returning to camp at Basingstoke on the latter date.

Lieut. R. J. H. Shaw was promoted Captain on 10th June, vice Major A. W. H. Bell, transferred to the 8th Shropshire Light Infantry.

A draft of 72 men from the 7th Royal Inniskilling Fusiliers joined the Battalion in camp at Basingstoke on the 12th June. These men had been transferred from the 16th Division to bring the units of the 10th Division up to strength. They were hurriedly put through a course of musketry at Aldershot.

The Rangers left Basingstoke in Brigade on

the 17th June for field operations against the 11th Division, and returned on the 19th June at 10 a.m. These operations took place in the neighbourhood of Holybourne, Alton, and Frensham.

On the 25th June a new pattern ' 1914 ' equipment made in England was issued to the Battalion, and that issued at the Curragh was immediately withdrawn.

2nd Lieut. G. Mortimer left the Battalion for Kinsale on the 28th June.

Lieut. J. W. Cartmel-Robinson rejoined on the 28th June, vice Lieut. Mortimer, who was transferred to the Reserve Battalion.

On the 27th June the 29th Brigade was ordered to hold itself in readiness for service in the Dardanelles.

All officers' chargers were given in to the Remount Department, and notification was received that the Transport Officer (2nd Lieut. A. C. Holmes, who had relieved 2nd Lieut. Fogarty), Transport Sergeant, and 20 drivers were to remain behind on the departure of the Battalion.

II

RECORD OF THE 5TH (SERVICE) BATTALION THE CONNAUGHT RANGERS

FROM 1ST JULY, 1915, TO 1ST OCTOBER, 1915.

THE 5th Battalion the Connaught Rangers was encamped at Basingstoke on the 1st July, 1915, when orders arrived officially warning the Battalion for service in the campaign then being waged on the Peninsula. Helmets and khaki drill clothing were at once issued to the men, and the process of fitting was completed by the 4th July. On the 6th July, orders for the embarkation of the Brigade were received, and on the following day the 10th Hampshire Regiment and the 6th Royal Irish Rifles entrained for the port of embarkation. On the 8th July the Battalion, less 12 officers and 159 other ranks—who left Basingstoke at 11 p.m. with Divisional Headquarters and other units for embarkation on H.M. Transport   at Liverpool under Captain B. R. Cooper—paraded in two parties at 8 p.m. and 10 p.m.

The first party comprised 9 officers and 397 other ranks under Lieut.-Colonel H. F. N. Jourdain commanding, and headquarters, marched to the London and South-Western Railway Station at

1915 Basingstoke, and, entraining in a few minutes, left at 9.10 p.m. for Keyham Dockyard.

The second party, also comprising 9 officers and 397 other ranks, left by the 11.40 p.m. train, under Major H. J. Nolan-Ferrall. These trains were due to arrive at Devonport at 5.50 a.m. and 8.20 a.m. on the 9th July.

Seven men of the 6th Leinster Regiment and 4 of the 10th Hampshire Regiment, together with 19 wagons, accompanied the Battalion on H.M. Transport   . The embarkation was completed by 10.50 a.m., and all stores and baggage were on board by that hour. At 1.20 p.m. the transport began to move out of the basin, and at 3.35 p.m. gained the open sea, escorted by H.M.S. *Medea* and *Mansfield*. As the vessel moved down the harbour the boys on the training-ships gave the Rangers a rousing cheer, and the drums of the Battalion played ' Brian Boru ' and other Irish tunes.

The weather was fine and warm and the troops were in splendid spirits.

Lieut.-Colonel Jourdain commanded the troops on board ship.

The   steered a ' zigzag ' course, and this was also done by the escorting destroyers, who continued to accompany the   until 8.20 a.m. on the 10th July, when they returned to their base at Devonport.

On the 10th July, after inspection of the ship at 10.30 a.m., the following message from His Majesty The King to the 10th Division was read by Lieut.-Colonel Jourdain :—

' Officers, non-commissioned officers and men.
You are about to join your comrades at the front
in bringing to a successful end this relentless war
of eleven months' duration. Your prompt patriotic answer to the nation's call to arms will never
be forgotten. The keen exertions of all ranks
during the period of training have brought you to
a state of efficiency not unworthy of my Regular
Army. I am confident that you will nobly uphold
the traditions of the fine Regiments whose names
you bear. Ever since your enrolment I have closely
watched the growth and steady progress of all
units. I shall continue to follow with interest
the fortunes of your Division. In bidding you
farewell, I pray that God may bless you in all your
undertakings.'

At the conclusion of the message, Lieut.-Colonel
Jourdain called for three cheers for His Majesty
The King, which were heartily given by all ranks.

The following officers accompanied the Battalion
on board the   :—

Lieut.-Colonel H. F. N. Jourdain (in command).
Major H. J. Nolan-Ferrall.
Major N. C. K. Money.
Captain A. S. Hog.
Captain A. Webber.
Captain B. W. Bond.
Captain R. J. H. Shaw.
Lieut. S. H. Lewis.
Lieut. R. R. Martin.
Lieut. J. W. Cartmel-Robinson.
2nd Lieut. H. T. Godber.
2nd Lieut. E. J. G. Kelly.

1915   2nd Lieut. G. R. Bennett.

2nd Lieut. J. Wallace.

Captain and Adjutant H. B. W. Maling.

Lieut. and Quartermaster P. Farrell.

Lieut. J. I. O'Sullivan, R.A.M.C. (Medic Officer), and the Rev. T. J. O'Connor, Roma Catholic Chaplain to the Forces (attached).

There were in all 18 officers and 786 oth ranks on board, with Sergt.-Major John Hudso the Reg.-Sergt.-Major of the Battalion.

The transport was one of the Elder Dempst Line, of 3,259 tonnage.

The Commanding Officer, previous to the depa ture of the Battalion from Basingstoke, issued t following order, which was read on parade by companies, and was afterwards inserted in t Battalion Records :—

' To all Companies of the 5th (Service) Battali the Connaught Rangers. Upon the eve of t departure of the Battalion on active service, a on the completion of nearly eleven months continuous and very exacting training for wa the Commanding Officer is very pleased to co gratulate all officers, warrant and non-comm sioned officers and men of the 5th Battalion t Connaught Rangers on the splendid condition the Battalion, and on the very loyal and efficie way they have all worked throughout the peri since the Battalion was formed. The Battali has earned for itself the highest commendati from Major-General Friend, C.B., Commandi the Forces in Ireland, Lieut.-General Sir Bry Mahon, and the Brig.-General Commanding t

Brigade ; and the good reports of all the Generals under which the Battalion has served have been very well earned. With the exception of the offence of absence, which has been all too frequent, the behaviour of the men has been very good indeed. The Commanding Officer wishes to convey to all ranks that it has been a great pleasure to command so fine a Battalion, and to have worked so harmoniously during the last eleven months with such splendid officers and men as the Battalion now possesses. He wishes to inform all ranks that he has subscribed from Battalion Funds to all Societies and Funds which have been helping the relatives and men of the Connaught Rangers. These Societies help both those who have lost relatives in the war, and those who have been wounded or who are prisoners of war, and all these committees will now help any Connaught Ranger of the 5th Battalion who may need their assistance. Any information on the subject can be always obtained from the officer commanding the dépôt at Galway or from the C.O. himself. It will be some satisfaction to know that the N.C.O.s and men of the 5th Battalion have not and will not be neglected. In conclusion, the C.O. wishes to especially thank those officers, warrant and non-commissioned officers and men, who since the raising of the Battalion have toiled unselfishly and successfully to make the Battalion what it now is. He would like to single out Sergt.-Major Hudson, who has done so much for the Battalion by his great zeal and unswerving loyalty, and who has shown such admirable tact throughout a particularly trying time.   The ready and efficient co-operation of all ranks has made the Battalion a highly trained and well-disciplined unit, of which all Battalions of the Connaught Rangers will indeed be proud.

'(Sd.) H. F. N. JOURDAIN,

'Lieut.-Colonel.

'O.C. 5th (Service) Bn. the Connaught Rangers. Basingstoke, 8th July, 1915.'

The following officers proceeded in the under Captain B. R. Cooper :—

Captain F. C. Burke.

Captain G. J. B. E. Massy.

Lieut. A. J. W. Blake.

Lieut. F. J. Charlton.

Lieut. T. S. P. Martin.

Lieut. O. M. Tweedy.

2nd Lieut. A. St. J. Mahony.

2nd Lieut. J. E. Burke.

2nd Lieut. A. D. Mulligan.

2nd Lieut. T. W. G. Johnson.

2nd Lieut. C. F. B. Harvey.

Together with 159 N.C.O.s and men, mostly of A Company (Captain Cooper's Company).

On the 11th July the Rev. T. J. O'Connor, C.F., celebrated mass at 7 a.m. on the after-deck, while the Church of England service was read by Major Money.

On the 14th July the   reached Gibraltar at 7 p.m., and proceeded on towards Malta at 7.30 p.m. the same date.   The weather was fine, and the run of the transport averaged about 230

miles every 24 hours. Tobacco and cigarettes
were served out to the men every other day, and
were very much appreciated by them.

On Sunday, the 18th July, the Rev. T. J.
O'Connor celebrated mass at 7 a.m., and at 6 p.m.
the same date read the funeral service over
Private Whyte, who died at sea at 4 p.m. from
pneumonia, and who was buried at sea the same
evening.

On the 19th July the   reached Malta at
7 a.m., and moved into the Grand Harbour near
the Custom House. Here coaling was ordered at
once, but was suddenly suspended, and the vessel
was ordered to put to sea at 6 p.m. ; the destination being Alexandria.

On leaving Malta the sea was somewhat rough
and choppy, and the quarters occupied by the
men were intensely hot, as the portholes had to
be closed to keep out the sea water.

On the 23rd July the   arrived outside
the breakwater at Alexandria at 9.55 a.m., and
anchored in the harbour a short time afterwards.

Mass was celebrated on the transport at 7 a.m.,
and although the service was voluntary, every
man available attended.

In the evening the   moved into the docks,
as orders arrived for the Orderly Room Sergt.
(Q.M.-Sergt. Heaney) and four storemen with
all base kits and limber wagons, water-carts and
officers' mess cart to be left at Alexandria. At
12 o'clock on the 24th July the Battalion paraded
on the wharf near the   , and proceeded through
the principal streets of Alexandria for a route

march. No rifles or side-arms were taken, but the drums of the Battalion played in fine style, and at 1.20 p.m. the Rangers returned to the ship very hot and dusty, but very much the better for the march through the city.

Coaling was again indulged in, but at 7 a.m. on the following day (25th July) the   began to move out of dock, and proceeded in a north-westerly direction towards the Island of Lemnos. At 11.30 a.m. mass for the troops was celebrated on board by the Chaplain.

The men were now clothed in khaki drill only, as all spare kits were left behind at Alexandria. The weather was now hot, but very pleasant, and the men were well supplied with pipes, cigarettes, and tobacco, which had been brought out with the Battalion from England.

At 6 a.m. on the 28th July, the   entered the harbour of Mudros, and anchored inside the boom at 6.15 a.m. and waited for instructions. At 9.30 a.m. the transport was ordered to move up to the inner harbour, and at 10.20 a.m. anchored for the second time near the French lines, north-west of the harbour.

At 5.20 p.m. urgent orders came for the to steam towards the South Pier (Turk's Head), but as the transport   was moored close along-side, this was not done until nearly 6.20 p.m. At 7 p.m. anchor was again let down near the South Pier, and orders were received for the disembarka-tion to commence at 8.15 a.m. on the 29th July. The work of disembarkation began punctually at the appointed hour, B and part of A Companies proceeding on shore with the first boats, followed soon afterwards by C and D Companies. Each man carried two days' rations and an iron ration. All baggage and officers' kits were loaded on the barges at 9.30 a.m. The companies as soon as they landed were marched up to the bivouac laid out for the Battalion, and here the headquarters of A Company and the officers and men who had proceeded in the   were encamped. The whole of the day (29th July) was spent in carrying by hand all the stores, officers' kit, baggage and rations from the pier to the bivouacking ground, as no transport at all was available.

The day was intensely hot, and the Battalion bivouac was nearly a mile distant from the South Pier. The day following the Battalion was instructed in drill, but on the 31st July Divisional night operations were the order. The heat was now very oppressive, and the swarms of flies and sand made bivouacking anything but pleasant.

The Battalion paraded at 9.20 p.m. on that day, and marched down towards the village of Pisperaghan, the 6th Leinster Regiment leading, followed by the 5th Battalion the Connaught Rangers, the 6th Royal Irish Rifles, and the 10th Hampshire Regiment. After a short halt at the village of Pisperaghan, the Brigade moved towards a high ridge; the men carrying ammunition, tools, and all equipment. At 2 a.m. the Battalion was ordered to halt on a high ridge about five miles from the bivouac, the men having done no march-

ing for over three weeks, and being very much
weakened by the severe attacks of dysentery,
which had forced about 10 per cent. of the
available strength to report sick.

At 2.45 a.m. the 'Cease fire' sounded, and the
troops marched back across very rough and
broken country to their camp.

The day had been insufferably hot, and water
was very scarce, and could only be obtained in
fixed quantities.

The Rangers remained at Mudros until the
5th August, when they were ordered to be ready
to embark at 10.30 a.m. at Turk's Head (South
Pier). The 6th Royal Irish Rifles proceeded
down to the shore, followed by the 10th Hampshire Regiment, and then the 6th Leinster
Regiment, and lastly the Rangers at the time
appointed.

On the previous day Captain B. W. Bond,
Lieut. F. J. Charlton, 2nd Lieut. C. F. B. Harvey,
and 176 N.C.O.s and men left the Battalion and
joined No. 12 Base Dépôt (then being formed)
as first reinforcement.

The Battalion fell in at 9.30 a.m. on the 5th
August and reached the South Pier at 10 a.m.,
only to find the other three regiments of the
Brigade still awaiting embarkation.

Hour after hour went by, while the pinnaces
and boats made trips backwards and forwards
to the troop carriers, but it was not until 3 p.m.
that the Rangers began to march to the pier and
commenced to embark.

The numbers embarking on the 5th August

were 25 officers and 749 other ranks. At 3.25 p.m.
the whole Battalion was on board the   ,
with one Company of the 6th Leinster Regiment,
and at 4 p.m. the   proceeded to sea,
calling at the   for orders.

After a smooth passage the transport anchored
at 10.20 p.m. outside Anzac Cove, but it was not
until after 3 a.m. on the morning of the 6th
August that the work of disembarkation began.
Then it was a race to get the men on land before
the day broke. During this time the bullets,
which either whistled harmlessly over the decks
or fell into the water near the   , claimed
two victims, one man of the Leinster Regiment
being shot in the chest, and one man of the
Rangers being wounded in the hand. The first
lighter full of men reached the pier at 3.45 a.m.,
and the men were ordered to disembark at once,
and following a New Zealand guide proceeded
to Shrapnel Gully with all haste. Not a moment,
however, was lost; as boatload after boatload
reached the pier the men quickly leapt ashore
and formed up under the sandy bluff near the
sea. The first party reached Shrapnel Gully at
4.30 a.m., and found that the rest of the 29th
Brigade had already began to dig themselves in
there.

Before the whole of the Battalion had reached
' Rest Gully ', as it was termed, in addition to
the name of ' Shrapnel Gully ', the enemy began
to shell the sap with shrapnel, but only one man
was slightly wounded in the shoulder.

There were many small holes in the part of

the gully allotted to the Rangers, which had been excavated by previous occupants, but few of these were shell-proof. The sound of rifle fire was at this time very heavy and incessant, both from the Turkish trenches and from those manned by the Australians, and when added to the sound of gun and machine-gun fire which broke out soon after the arrival of the Battalion, the noise was quite deafening. Sleep was impossible, and the plague of flies made rest in a ' dug-out ' a matter quite out of the question. However, the men were ordered to take as much rest as possible until 4 a.m. on the following morning. At 11 a.m. on this date (6th August) heavy rifle fire broke out, and a quarter of an hour later a shell fell into a ' dug-out ' and killed a man named Private Hall of C Company. Only a few minutes later Q.M.-Sergt. Galbraith and another man were slightly wounded by shrapnel. On the other side of the gully a shell burst in the precincts of the Hampshire Regiment. The sound of gun-fire died down about 1.30 p.m., but at 3 p.m. shelling recommenced again, and several men were hit, but not seriously wounded.

At 4.30 p.m. Lieut.-Colonel Jourdain went to the Brigade Headquarters for orders, and while maps were being issued to the C.O.s of the Brigade, the bombardment of the enemy's position began. At 5.30 p.m. the enemy's lines on the Lone Pine plateau were attacked and taken. Shrapnel and bullets from the Turkish trenches, which passed over the Australian lines, fell into the gully where the 29th Brigade were resting, and the incessant

splash of the bullets on the sandy hillside re-
sembled a hailstorm on a summer's day. 'Dug-
outs' were almost useless, but the men bore their
baptism of fire quite splendidly. As night closed
in, the fire from both sides redoubled and the
noise of gun and rifle fire was intense and unending. Cooking was out of the question that
night, and cold or rather warm water, biscuits
and tinned meat satisfied the cravings of hunger.

The Brigade was ordered to be ready to move
at 1 a.m., and all kits were packed in readiness
for that hour. The sound of musketry went on
although the shadows had fallen, and was never
silent throughout the entire night. During the day
the Rangers lost one man killed and nine wounded.

At 12.40 a.m. on the 7th August the Rangers
fell in and marched down towards the gully at
the bottom of the Shrapnel Valley, the Leinster
Regiment and the Irish Rifles being in front in
the order named. The march was continued
slowly towards 'Monash Gully' and 'Quinn's
Post'. The night was extremely dark, but after
a short march the Brigade was halted, and the
6th Leinster Regiment were detailed to remain as
support, and were accordingly detached from the
Brigade. The remainder of the Brigade marched
back to the upper part of Bridges' Road.

At 4 a.m. the bombardment of the Turkish
position began again, and for a half-hour the
noise was deafening and incessant. The mass of
projectiles which were hurled against the hostile
position was terrific, and was more than enough
to try even the Turk, stout fighter though he be.

1915 The attack on the Lone Pine position had been successful, but the attack on the German officers' trench had been beyond the power of human endurance. During the night Corporal O'Brien was wounded in the chest by a bullet.

The Rangers waited on the Bridges' Road in case their services were required, and were subjected to some shrapnel fire, but although three officers were hit by splinters, they were not wounded. These officers were Captain Cooper, Captain Burke, and Lieut. Cartmel-Robinson.

The sickness, which had increased in an alarming manner after the arrival of the Battalion at Mudros, now grew less and less, and few men presented themselves to the Medical Officer, in case they should miss any service to which the Battalion might be allotted. Throughout the day the unending stream of dead and wounded men continued down the Bridges' Road, demonstrating the stern nature of the fighting that had been carried on by both sides since the previous evening. Many shells and missiles from trench mortars fell into the position occupied by the Battalion, but few men were even wounded.

At 7 p.m. the 5th Rangers were suddenly ordered to dispatch one Company to near Brown's Dip, and the remainder of the Battalion were ordered to proceed to reinforce the 1st Australian Brigade. The position was reached at 8.10 p.m., and the Rangers occupied quarters on the hillside near the 12th Australian Infantry, under Brig.-General Sinclair MacLagan, D.S.O., and facing due south and the headland of Gaba Tepe. During

the day two men of the Battalion were wounded.
B Company, under Major Money, proceeded to
near Brown's Dip, while A, C, and D remained
with headquarters.

Darkness soon compelled a short cessation of
hostilities, and many who had had no sleep for
two nights, although without any covering what-
soever, slept soundly until awakened by a heavy
bombardment at 3 a.m. on the 8th August, which
heralded the arrival of the early dawn.   At
6 a.m. all ranks partook of a frugal breakfast of
tea without however sugar, and jam and biscuit.
One man of A Company was wounded in the leg
early in the day. Several of the hostile shells fell
among the Battalion, but did little damage.
Meanwhile B Company had been employed all
night in clearing the trenches and carrying down
and burying the dead, and had one casualty,
Private Kelleher, who was wounded in the foot.

Throughout the day the sound of gun-fire
from destroyers, monitors and other ships, as
well as from the land batteries, went on continuously, and several shells fell among the
bivouacs of the companies of the Rangers. At
11.30 a.m. Major Money reported several men
wounded in his Company.

The day passed without incident until 6 p.m.,
when orders arrived for the three headquarters
companies to move down to Victoria Gully.
The Battalion paraded at once and moved down
to their allotted position, and, although the day
was far advanced, companies were ordered to
dig themselves in as quickly as possible. During

the day Lieut. Cartmel-Robinson and 14 men were wounded, and Lieut. T. S. P. Martin and 2nd Lieut. T. W. G. Johnson were both struck by spent bullets, but did not report sick.

Early on the morning of the 9th August B Company was ordered to rejoin headquarters, as the Battalion was ordered to be ready to rejoin the 29th Brigade. At 9 a.m., however, the order was cancelled and the Battalion was ordered to remain at Victoria Gully. C Company, under Captain Hog, proceeded up to near Brown's Dip to take the place of B Company. A few minutes past eleven 3 of C Company were brought down severely wounded. Scarce an hour had elapsed since these men had gone up both cheery and willing for any work. The sound of gun-fire from the left of the Anzac position was both continuous and heavy during the morning, and in the evening the enemy shelled the cutting just below where the Battalion was stationed, killing and wounding many of the Mule Corps and baggage animals. In the evening orders were received for the Battalion to be ready to reinforce the front line, if necessary.

During the night D Company went up to relieve C Company, which had suffered a loss of 1 man killed and 8 wounded during the day. 2nd Lieut. T. W. G. Johnson had been brought prominently to notice for having twice bound up men's wounds under heavy fire, and for having behaved with great gallantry in holding an advanced trench. The behaviour of all ranks during this trying time was beyond praise, and the work done by B and C Companies was excellent. D Company also did very well indeed.

At 7 a.m. on the 10th August, orders arrived for the Battalion to concentrate and move at once to Anzac Cove and there obtain orders. D Company was recalled immediately, and rejoined headquarters at 7.53 a.m. All water-bottles were at once filled, and the Battalion prepared to move to the left or almost due north.

During the short time that D Company had been on duty at the front trenches, they had sustained the loss of five men wounded. They had practically no sleep all night, and had only been withdrawn a short time before the Battalion paraded and marched away. Their spirit was, however, excellent. Led by Major Nicholson, the G.S.O. III. of the Australian and New Zealand Army Corps, the Rangers made a large détour to escape the observation of the enemy from Gaba Tepe, and reached Anzac Cove at 9 a.m. without a casualty. At Anzac the Battalion was ordered to take on 3,000 sandbags and to push on towards No. 2 Post. The day was exceedingly hot and there was no breeze, the sandy shore of the Anzac beach gave anything but a sure foothold to those who had been continuously employed throughout the preceding night, but there was no halting, as the services of the Battalion were sorely needed. The Rangers now entered the sap, which led to No. 2 Post, but the stream of wounded men made progress extremely difficult, and at 10.15 a.m. the head of the Battalion emerged from the sap and reported at No. 2 Post for orders. Here were

1915 assembled Lieut.-General Sir W. R. Birdwood ar
Major-Generals Sir A. Godley and F. Shaw, wh
informed Lieut.-Colonel Jourdain that the Turl
had massed and driven in part of the line, ar
urged him to push on and report to Brig.-Gener
H. V. Cox, C.B., C.S.I., as soon as possible.

The Battalion also heard with much regret th;
the Brigadier had been grievously wounded, ar
that Lieut.-Colonels Bradford, Craske, and Bewshe
and the Brigade Major had been stricken dow
The men had marched grandly in the terrific hea
and had been under arms since 7 a.m., but the
responded splendidly to the call, and as soon as tl
tail of the column was clear of the sap, the advan
was continued without halt or check. Not a sing
man lingered by the way, or fell out even for
second, although the long line of bloodstain
wounded and dying men, which at times almc
barred the passage through the sap, was more th;
enough to appal the stoutest heart.

The orders from the New Zealand and Australi;
Division were as follows :—

' O.C. Connaught Rangers.

' N.Z.G. 152—10th August.

' Your Battalion will proceed at once up t
Aghyl Dere and come under the orders of Brigadi(
General Cox, commanding the 6th Section
Defence. General Cox is sending an officer
meet you to guide and give you orders, AA
You should halt the head of your column at t
junction of the Aghyl Dere square 92 X.Y.

'(Sd.) W. G. BRAITHWAITE.'

Pushing rapidly on, the Rangers passed the Chilak Dere and Bauchop's Hill, and then striking in a north-easterly direction, entered the Aghyl Dere, and in accordance with instructions the head of the Battalion was halted at the junction of the two branches of the Aghyl Dere soon after 11 a.m.

Progress up the dried-up water-course became very difficult, owing to the large numbers of wounded men who lay by the bank of the Dere waiting to be transported down to the beach. Water, except at the few waterholes, was unobtainable, and the enemies' fire continually claimed a victim, even from among those that lay bleeding and helpless by the roadside.

General Cox's headquarters was reached at 11.15 a.m., and after the General had pointed out the present position of the Turkish force on the Chunak Bair, he gave Lieut.-Colonel Jourdain the following order :—

' O.C. Connaught Rangers.

' Am placing two companies of your Regiment at disposal G.O.C. 39th Brigade at 12.45 p.m., to reinforce his line. His headquarters are on hill just above you to left; bearer will show you— I have told him where to find you.

' (Sd.) H. V. Cox, Br.-Gen.'

12.20 p.m.

The Battalion was accordingly concentrated at 11.40 a.m., and the march up the Aghyl Dere was continued, until the headquarters of the 39th Brigade was reached, now under Brigadier-General W. de S. Cayley. Here the Rangers halted behind a hill, on which the headquarters of the 39th Briga was established.   The men of A and B Compan were ordered to advance, as soon as they had h teas, as only limited water was obtainable, and t men were parched with thirst and covered with du

These two companies were ordered to proceed the Aghyl Dere, and then up the steep wooc slopes of the Chunak Bair towards the Farm.

The G.O.C. wished the ridge just below t Farm, a small portion which was cultivated and which some corn was plainly seen, to be held, order that the wounded might be brought saf down and that the small detachments of t different corps then said to be clinging to the ric might be relieved and collected.   At 2.10 p. A and B Companies of the 5th Battalion co menced their arduous task.   These compan were commanded respectively by Captain B. Cooper and Major N. C. K. Money, and were st jected to heavy and continuous rifle fire, chie from snipers, as soon as they began to move fr their halting-place.   The enemy had posted snip right down the slope of the Chunak Bair, a several of these were found with branches of tr tied over their heads, even after the first line men had passed their hiding-places.   The slope the Hill was exceedingly steep, and in the sul afternoon was indeed a most formidable obstac even to troops which might have been unoppos The leading platoons, however, reached the rid but suffered a good many casualties during th advance ; the remainder were not long in joini their comrades.   At 4 p.m. Brigadier-Gene

Cayley pointed out from Brigade Headquarters the position he wished taken up at night, which was a low line of rocky underfeatures connecting the point held by the 7th (Service) Battalion North Stafford Regiment and the hill held by the 14th Sikhs. At 5.15 p.m. Major Money reported that he was still in occupation of slopes below right of Farm, but that every inch of ground was under fire, and that he had lost heavily at each corner and opening. General Cayley thereupon ordered the two companies to remain where they were for the present to cover the removal of the wounded and the withdrawal of scattered parties. After dark they were ordered to retire to the bottom of the slope and hold the spur on the left of the gully, which had been pointed out by the G.O.C., or until relieved by C and D Companies.

The position to be taken up at night was wholly commanded by the hostile machine-guns which had played such a prominent part in the fighting in the early morning, and which had accounted for so many casualties in Major Money's two companies on Chunak Bair. This position had a poor field of fire, besides entailing larger numbers for the defence than a shorter and better line through Green Hill and Sikh Hill would have done. The Brigadier-General commanding, however, wished this line taken up, and C and D Companies were detailed for this purpose.

A and B Companies had been doing splendid service all the afternoon collecting the various scattered parties of men, who had been in action since the early morning, and in succouring and

D

sending down the wounded lying below the Farm. Their losses were heavy, and in A Company Captain G. J. B. E. Massy and Lieuts. T. S. P. Martin and A. D. Mulligan had been wounded, although Captain Massy gallantly remained in the firing line until it was recalled in the evening, when he accompanied it back to headquarters.

After A and B Companies had reached their bivouac, Major Money and many volunteers from those companies went out again and again and personally brought in all wounded men outside the line. Many of the stretcher-bearers worked on throughout the night, and before dawn on the following day all those who had been wounded during that terrible day's fighting were either sent down to the dressing station or were safely within our lines. The greatest devotion to duty was shown by the medical officer of the Battalion—Lieut. J. I. O'Sullivan, R.A.M.C., who toiled unceasingly throughout a most trying period, and did not desist before all the wounded had been attended to.

The steadiness of the men during this critical and trying time, and their willingness for any duty, surpassed all expectations, and the gallant behaviour of the officers of those companies was beyond all praise.

At 6.10 p.m. C and D Companies under Captain Hog and Captain Webber paraded and marched out to take up the outpost line which had been ordered by the G.O.C. 39th Brigade. They were at once subjected to a heavy rifle fire, and although they reached the spur in front of and north-east of Green Hill, they found that these two companies would be unable to hold it, as the enemy brought machine-gun fire at once to bear upon it, which enfiladed the proposed line of resistance.

Captain Maling, the adjutant, having reported the result of his reconnaissance, and Lieut.-Colonel Jourdain, after acquainting the Brigadier-General with the situation, the two companies were withdrawn to an inner line, which was at once fortified, and before daylight rendered quite impregnable.

The work done by C Company on Green Hill was very good indeed, and a splendid line of defence was thrown up in an incredibly short space of time. The casualties during the day had been heavy, and even when darkness fell the wounded continued to swell the large numbers who had been brought in by the men of the Rangers, and lay awaiting the dressing by the medical officer.

At one time no less than 320 men, of nearly every Battalion in the 13th Division and the 29th Brigade, were gathered together in a small space of open ground, with almost every kind of wound imaginable, many of whom had been grievously wounded in the early hours of the morning of the 10th August, and had had no treatment for their wounds, and were in addition parched with thirst. The gallant stretcher-bearers worked on and on, and it was late on the 11th before all the wounded were attended to and carried down to the beach, where some better attention and food could be given them. 2nd Lieut. Wallace was wounded the same night.

The Battalion stood to arms an hour before dawn on the 11th August, but no advance was made by the enemy. There were, however, no supports available, and a strong attack by the enemy would have had to be borne by the first line alone. Many of the Battalions of the 13th Division had lost nearly all their officers, and the men were quite worn out with their exertions. The Brigadier-General decided during the course of the morning of the 11th August to depute the Rangers to seize the spur which had been selected as the original line of defence. During the afternoon the enemy shelled the position held by C Company, but with only a few casualties. Heavy sniping, however, went on all day long, and several men were wounded in the front trenches. The day was again insufferably hot, and the scarcity of water, which militated against any advance, was most cheerfully borne by the men. In addition to these discomforts the odour of many human corpses, which lay unburied in the vicinity, made the atmosphere almost unbearable. Burying parties were organized as soon as evening fell, and all arms, ammunition, and equipment were collected and sent down to Brigade Headquarters as quickly as possible.

The advance on the ridge in front of the line then held by the Rangers was timed to commence at 9 p.m. that night. A and B Companies, augmented by one platoon of D Company, under Major Money, composed the force destined to seize and hold the position. This operation was splendidly carried out by Major Money, and without expending a round of ammunition the ridge was carried with the bayonet with the loss of two men wounded. The enemy, who had occupied the spur with small parties, were either bayoneted or put to flight, and the line was at once fortified and consolidated. This was firmly held throughout the ensuing day, although the enemy sent forward numbers of snipers to annoy those working on the line.

Lieut.-Colonel Jourdain was ordered on the 11th August to assume command of the 29th Brigade, he being the senior officer left in the Brigade, after Brig.-General Cooper, Lieut.-Colonel Bradford, and Lieut.-Colonel Craske had been wounded; and on the 12th August proceeded down to Olive Grove and took over command of the Brigade. Major Money assumed temporary command of the Battalion on the same date.

On the morning of the 12th August Captain A. S. Hog was severely wounded, and to the regret of all ranks afterwards died at sea of wounds received in action on that day.

Fifteen men were also wounded during the day (12th August).

On the evening of the 13th August the Battalion was relieved from duty in the advanced trenches, and was brought down to the Olive Grove to rest. A and B Companies arrived at 10.30 p.m., and were followed some hours afterwards by C and D Companies.

Lieut.-Colonel Agnew, M.V.O., D.S.O., 3rd Royal Scots Fusiliers, arrived to take over command of the 29th Brigade, and Lieut.-Colonel Jourdain resumed command of the Battalion from the same date (13th August).

Although the 5th Battalion had had continuous duty either in the trenches or in attack since their arrival on the Peninsula, and had been moved to the Olive Grove, in order to give the men a well-earned rest, no sooner had the last platoons of C and D Companies reached the Battalion Head-quarters, in the early hours of the 14th August, than urgent requisitions for fatigues came from all sides.   Several fatigues were provided for digging the sap down to the Aghyl Dere, and down to the Waterhole, but at length some protest was neces-sary, and the Rangers were called upon for no more duties, and the men were given as much rest as possible for that day.   Rifle fire and sniping was exceedingly heavy even in the early morning, and orders were given for the men to dig themselves in as quickly as possible to save losses.   At 2 p.m. on the 14th August the Battalion was warned to be ready to move to the flank of the Indian Brigade and to be stationed in échelon on the flank to act as flank guard to the 9th Corps, which was stated to be preparing for a further advance at dawn on the morrow.   The orders detailed the Rangers to lead the advance, and the 6th Battalion Royal Irish Rifles, which were to be brought up from fatigue on the beach, to act in support.

These orders were cancelled soon afterwards, at 5.47 p.m., and the Battalion remained in bivouac in the Olive Grove.

The day did not, however, pass without loss : one man who exposed himself on the crest line was killed immediately, and six men of D Company were wounded in the trenches at the top of the slight eminence overlooking the Grove, and during the night two more men were wounded.

During the night, parties told off for the purpose worked unceasingly throughout the night at the sap down to the Aghyl Dere, and an excellent piece of work it became.

The Chaplains to the Brigade had not yet joined from Mudros, where they had been attached to the 30th Field Ambulance, but the Rev. Father Leighton, who has since been awarded the Military Cross, and who had done splendid work in the Dere close by, volunteered to come up and see the men of the Rangers. His offer was accepted with great pleasure by the Commanding Officer, and he came up on the same evening, and cele-brated mass the following morning (the 15th August).

Even on the afternoon of the 14th August, while the priest was hearing confessions, the bullets continually struck the trees or the sandy bluff close by, and one poor fellow was brought down with a gaping wound in the forehead. He was dead, but he had died a soldier's death, and all ranks were sorry to lose him. His name was Reynolds.

On Sunday, the 15th August, mass was cele-brated by Rev. W. Leighton at 5.20 a.m. in the C.O.'s 'Dugout', and scarce had the service concluded when death claimed another victim, who had only received communion a quarter of an hour before. A hasty grave was dug, and he was buried almost at once. The sound of heavy rifle fire had come from the east, and many bullets fell among the Battalion with but little loss. On the previous afternoon Major-General Shaw, C.B., had visited the Rangers in their bivouac in the Olive Grove. The Battalion now had two posts overlooking the camp, and four working parties, otherwise the remainder of the Regiment was concentrated.

It was arranged that the Rangers were under the orders of Brig.-General Cayley for ' tactics ', but for any other duties they were under Lieut.-Colonel Agnew, M.V.O., D.S.O., 3rd Royal Scots Fusiliers. The Battalion sustained the loss of two men killed on the 15th and several wounded at the barricade, as well as one man wounded at the post overlooking the camp.

On the 16th August the Battalion was inspected by Lieut.-Colonel Agnew, who then visited the posts over the camp.

The following names were sent in by the Commanding Officer for gallant and distinguished service on the 8th, 9th, and 10th August :—

Major N. C. K. Money, for gallantry in covering the retirement of detachments from the slopes of the Chunak Bair and for personal bravery in bringing down the wounded under a heavy fire. This officer rendered splendid service on the 10th August, 1915, on the above service, and although followed by Turkish snipers did not desist before all the wounded were brought in.

Captain B. R. Cooper handled his Company splendidly both in attack and in bringing it out of action on the 10th August.

Captain and Adjutant H. B. W. Maling, for good service on the 10th and 11th August, 1915, during the operations near the Aghyl Dere.

Captain G. J. B. E. Massy, although wounded in the arm, continued in the firing line all the afternoon of the 10th August on the Chunak Bair, and displayed conspicuous gallantry in covering the bringing away of the wounded and in organizing the defence of the ridge under a heavy machinegun fire.

2nd Lieut. A. D. Mulligan behaved with great gallantry on the 10th August at the Chunak Bair, and rendered most efficient service until wounded.

No. 3,010, Reg.-Sergt.-Major John Hudson, has behaved with conspicuous gallantry on the 10th and 11th August in the operations near the Aghyl Dere, which has in my opinion been highly commendable, and three times on the above dates volunteered for and carried through minor operations, although exposed to a severe cross-fire on each occasion. This warrant officer has already won the Distinguished Conduct Medal.

2nd Lieut. T. W. G. Johnson behaved with conspicuous gallantry on the 8th August at Lone Pine in binding up an officer's wounds under heavy fire, and for great courage during the 8th and 9th August.

No. 5/83, Private J. Geehan, remained with a wounded officer under heavy machine-gun fire on the 10th August, and did not retire before he brought him back to the dressing station.

No. 5/3831, Private J. Sweeney, behaved with great gallantry on the 10th August in the Aghyl Dere in proceeding across a bullet-swept area to warn other soldiers, and thus saving the lives of many of his comrades.

No. 5/529, Private M. Kilroy, for great gallantry and devotion to duty on the 10th and 11th August 1915, in bringing in the wounded and in crossing a fire-swept zone to bring in wounded men. This he did several times, and displayed the most conspicuous gallantry.

No. 5/3355, Private J. Horgan, twice ran out under machine-gun fire on the 12th August to bring in a comrade who had fallen and was unable to rise.

No. 5/604, Lance-Corporal Charles McDonald, for conspicuous bravery and devotion to duty when employed as stretcher-bearer in bringing in wounded under a galling fire, thereby saving many lives on the 10th and 11th August in the neighbourhood of the Aghyl Dere.

These recommendations were sent in to Brigade Headquarters on the 16th August.

The Battalion was warned this day to be ready to take over the trenches then held by the 6th (Service) Battalion South Lancashire Regiment and the 6th (Service) Battalion East Lancashire Regiment on the 17th August.

At 9 p.m. one man was killed by a sniper. At 10.55 p.m. orders came for one officer and 50 men of the Battalion to relieve the post of the 6th Royal Irish Rifles on Ghurkha Post. These rejoined the Battalion the next day. The enemy as usual indulged in sniping the posts round the bivouac, and many bullets fell in the lines throughout the night.

At 7.50 p.m. on the 17th August the Battalion paraded under what cover was available, and this was very meagre, and marched in single file up the Aghyl Dere water-course, and took over the trenches held by the Service Battalions of the East Lancashire and South Lancashire Regiments. The relief was complete before 9 p.m., and the relieved regiments left soon after that hour.

The Regiment as usual stood to arms an hour before daybreak, on the 18th August, and then continued the improvement of the trenches which had been commenced the previous evening. Brig.-General Cayley and Lieut.-Colonel Agnew complimented the Battalion on the improvement in the lines. The day was spent in working at all the trenches with excellent results, and except for one man who was seriously wounded, there were no further casualties.

At 8.40 p.m. the New Zealanders rushed a Turkish trench on Rhododendron Spur, but were compelled to relinquish it later. This trench was about a mile in front of the Rangers' lines. Early on the morning of the 19th August one man was killed, and one acting Company Q.M.-Sergeant, one Sergeant, one Corporal, and one man were wounded in the trenches, chiefly in those of D Company, who were stationed to the left and upon whose working parties the enemy brought a machine-gun. A continual hail of bullets came over the trenches the previous night, but happily no one was wounded.

Some rain fell in the early morning, but scarcely laid the dust, which lay thick on the pathways up to the trenches. The sound of heavy gun-fire went on all day long, and the enemy's snipers pressed forward to the trenches held by the Rangers, until driven back by picked shots who crept out of a tunnel made under the parapet and effectually caused a retirement of the enemy's picked shots.

One man was killed and four wounded this day.

On the 20th August the Battalion as usual stood to arms before dawn, the early morning being extremely cold for all ranks, clothed only in khaki drill with no coats or covering other than what they stood up in.

At 6.20 a.m. orders were received for the Rangers to be relieved from the trenches soon after midday, and then to be ready to move this day to join Major-General Cox's Brigade. The exact hour was notified later. The 5th Battalion having been relieved by two units of the 13th Division, the Rangers left the trenches on ' Lancashire Hill ' at 2.40 p.m., and marched to the bivouac in Olive Grove, which was reached about 18 minutes later. Major-General Cox had expressed a desire that the Battalion should be allowed to take as much rest as possible, in view of the strenuous work which the Regiment was to be called upon to perform on the morrow.

The Commanding Officer and Major Money

proceeded at 4.30 p.m. to the Headquarters of
the 29th Brigade, and afterwards, at 5.20 p.m.,
proceeded to the Headquarters of the 29th Indian
Brigade.   The position held by the Turks near
Kabak Kuyu was pointed out, and the plans for
the attack were explained by Major-General Cox
to Brigadier-General Russell, Lieut.-Colonel Agnew,
and Lieut.-Colonel Jourdain, commanding the 5th
Battalion the Connaught Rangers.   The bivouac
of the Battalion was reached at 7.10 p.m., and the
companies paraded at once to march to their new
bivouac at ' South Wales Borderers' Gully ', near
' Gillespie Hill '.

The march was commenced as soon as darkness
fell, to conceal the movement of the troops, as it
was necessary to cross some open ground, which
was completely in view of the Turkish position on
the Sari Bair.   Very silently the head of the
column began to move at 8.20 p.m. down the
Aghyl Dere, and then up to where the Headquarters
of the 29th Indian Brigade had been on the 10th
August, and across the open cornfields towards
the low ridge of hills manned by the 4th (Service)
Battalion South Wales Borderers and the Damakjelik Bair.   A short halt had to be called to take
up bombs, sandbags, and entrenching tools near
the Brigade Headquarters, but otherwise the
column moved quietly on to their appointed
bivouac.   Not a sound went up, and not a man
spoke during this advance, and at 9 p.m. the
leading Company, which immediately followed the
Battalion Headquarters, reached the advanced
bivouac.   Here C Company were located for the

1915 night, and were followed immediately by D, A, and B, in the order named.

As C Company would be the first to advance on the morrow, they were placed in the most advanced bivouac, and the other companies as above stated. Officers and men in the waning moonlight soon lay down to rest and to prepare themselves for the stern work which lay before all the next day. At the express wish of the General there was no stand-to-arms on the morning of the 21st August, but at 8.15 a.m. the Commanding Officer pointed out the objective and the line of attack to the Company Officers and the Machine-gun Officer (Lieut. Lewis), who visited the trenches of the South Wales Borderers for that purpose.

A little later the other officers of the Battalion viewed the position to be assaulted from the trenches of the South Wales Borderers, through a periscope, as the hostile snipers were extremely persistent and prevented any one showing himself even for a moment over the parapet. Captain R. J. H. Shaw had joined the Staff of the 29th Brigade as Staff-Captain on the previous day.

Major-General Cox's force was divided into three sections : the left section to press forward and establish a permanent hold on the lightly-held outpost line covering the junction of the 11th Division with the left of the Anzac front ; the centre section (composed of the 5th Battalion Connaught Rangers, with one Company of the 4th South Wales Borderers with picks and shovels to consolidate the position when won) to seize

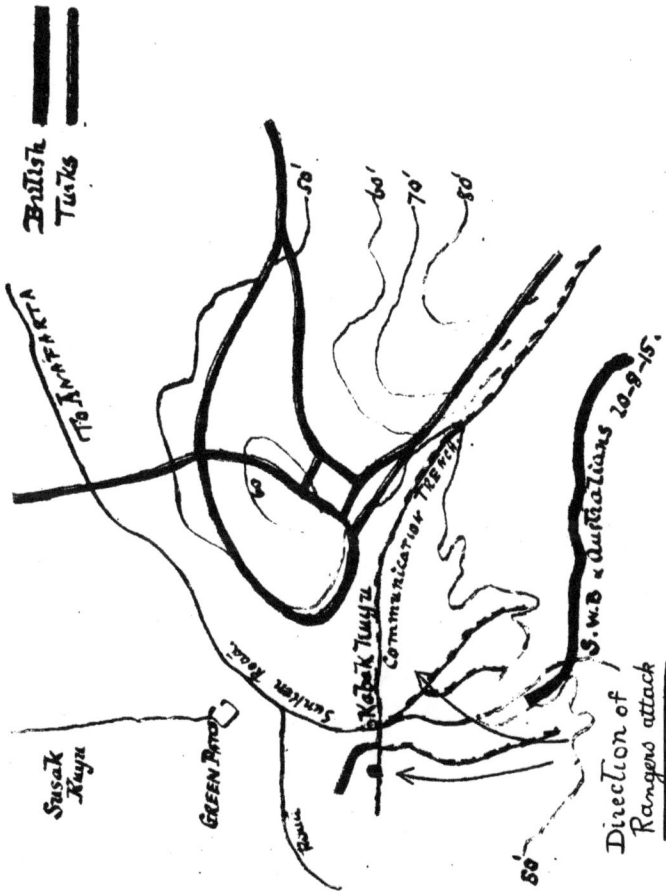

British ▬▬▬
Turks ══

Position of British and Turkish Trenches on 10th August 1915.
after a sketch by Major Brunby R.E.

Susak Kuyu

GREEN PATCH

Sarkan Road

TO ANAFARTA

Kabak Kuyu
COMMUNICATION TRENCH

S.W.B. & Australians 10-9-15.

Direction of
Rangers attack

50'
60'
70'
80'

50'

the wells at Kabak Kuyu, an asset of the utmost value, whether to our side or to the enemy; the right section to attack and capture the Turkish trenches on the north-east side of the Kaiajik Aghala. The Rangers were to debouch from the left of the lines held by the 4th South Wales Borderers and, advancing by a shallow water-course or gully some twenty-five yards across, and bordered on the left by a small hill held by the 14th Sikhs, and opposite that held by the South Wales Borderers, to advance directly on the two trenches held by the Turks some three hundred yards in front of the entrance of the gully. Slightly beyond these trenches lay the wells, which were situated almost at the junction of a large ' Sunken Road ', which led to Biyuk Anafarta and a large communication trench, which had been a water-course and which the Turks had now made a most useful communication trench, which con-nected with the Turkish trenches on the Hill 60 or Kaiajik Aghala.

The Rangers were ordered to co-operate with the right column under Brig.-General Russell, after the position assigned to them had been won.

The General wished the position to be taken at the point of the bayonet, and no man was to stop to fire until the trenches were gained. All packs, &c., were to be left behind in the bivouac of the previous night. One sandbag at least was carried by every man, and bombers were equipped with their haversacks and bags complete with bombs. Picks and shovels were assigned to the supporting companies, and one Company of the

1915 South Wales Borderers was ordered to follow up and to consolidate the position when won. The details of conducting the attack were left to the Commanding Officer, who drew up the orders for the attack, which were issued at 12 o'clock. At 11 a.m. the Rev. J. W. Crozier held a communion service for the soldiers belonging to the Church of England, and the Rev. T. J. O'Connor held a short service for those belonging to the Roman Catholic Church. Even while the men were thus engaged, the Turkish snipers were not inactive, and bullet after bullet ploughed up the dust but several yards away. After service the scheme and orders were explained minutely to all ranks, and every preparation to ensure success was made by the officers commanding the four companies of the Battalion. The spirit of the Fifth was beyond praise, and only those requiring some treatment to the many sores on their hands and arms appeared before the Medical Officer that day.

At 1.30 p.m. Major-General Sir Alexander Godley came to the bivouac and asked to see as many of the officers and N.C.O.s and men as possible. He made them a short and stirring speech, in which he informed them that one Regiment had attempted to take the wells and had failed, and he looked to the Rangers to do so [the murmurs of approval were at once suppressed] in a fashion that was known to all, by the cold steel and accompanied by an Irish yell. At the conclusion he shook hands with all the officers, and wished both them and the men ' God speed'. His words appealed to the gallant Irish soldiers to whom they were addressed, and it was with a grim resolution to do their duty fearlessly that they returned to their hot and sandy resting-place, to await the signal for the advance.

Major-General Cox and Lieut.-Colonel Agnew also were present to wish the Battalion the best of luck in their endeavour.

The Rangers paraded at 2 p.m. and began to move up the pathway which lay between the two low ridges, and which led up to the advanced position of the South Wales Borderers. Every attempt was made to keep the dust down, in case it should betray their presence to the enemy. The bombardment of the Turkish positions in front of the advance of the 9th Corps, and also on the Kaiajik Aghala and in the plain near Susak Kuyu, was to begin at 2.30 p.m., when all companies were to be in position.

Information now was sent round that the attack would be postponed from 3.10 to 3.40 p.m. The bombardment, however, went on at 2.30 p.m., and the country seemed buried in smoke and flame. The land batteries and the men-of-war off shore joined in this concentrated bombardment by land and sea on the enemy positions. Several parties of the enemy were seen to retire, but the occupants of the trenches near the wells showed themselves not at all. The earth seemed to quiver beneath the force of such tremendous explosions. The bombardment continued with only five minutes' intermission until 3.40 p.m. Scarcely had the fumes and the dust of the last

E

salvo died away, than the leading platoon of C Company, commanded by Captain B. W. Bond, issuing rapidly from the gorge from which the wire entanglements had been removed the previous night, shook out at once to four paces interval, and proudly as if on parade made for the advanced trenches. Nor were the other platoons to be out-distanced or left behind, and with a yell they too closed up at once and, preserving the most correct formation, vied with each other which should reach the objective first. They were, however, met with a burst of fire which was enough to appal the stoutest heart, but there was no hesitation. The utmost gallantry was shown by Captain Bond, 2nd Lieuts. J. E. Burke, Bennett, and Johnson, and by every man whom they led.

D Company, under Captain Webber, followed close behind, and moved out across the open ground towards the Green Patch and Susak Kuyu. The last platoon of C Company rushed towards the communication trench, which they quickly cleared, bombed out the occupants, and blocked same near the well, and above the junction with the Sunken Road. The other platoons with D Company quickly closed with the enemy, and it was swift stern work with the bayonet. The Turks remained to the last and fought it out, and with few exceptions, who were caught by our machine-gun fire up the sunken road, they perished almost to a man. 2nd Lieut. T. W. G. Johnson, entering a trench, bayoneted six Turks and then shot two more. He has been awarded the Military Cross for this deed and for his great bravery at the Lone Pine trenches.

The Rangers showed that their instruction in bayonet-fighting had not been forgotten, and the many Turkish snipers who remained behind and attempted to pick off the officers were not neglected. Even at the entrance to the gorge when the companies first broke cover, several of the enemy's marksmen were met with and paid the extreme penalty. The leading companies had easily taken the two foremost trenches before many minutes and were in possession of the Sunken Road, when A Company, under Captain F. C. Burke, was ordered forward at 4.25 p.m. to fill up a small gap between D and C Companies and to support the latter. This Company moved forward swiftly and carrying the first line with it captured another Turkish trench north-east of the Sunken Road on the slopes of the Kaiajik Aghala.

B Company moved up in support, and reached the Sunken Road soon after A Company, which began to advance beyond it, and up the slope to the Kaiajik Aghala. The objective was gained, the wells and their defences were in the hands of the Battalion, and the Rangers' advanced line was pushing on to assist Brig.-General Russell's attack when the enemy began to shell the advancing line. The trench which had been captured in front of the Sunken Road became at once untenable, through the machine-gun and shrapnel fire that had been brought to bear on it. Here there was no retreat, and the occupants

E 2

1915 died at their posts without exception. The
hostile gun-fire now became intense, and the
companies holding the Sunken Road were subjected to a severe bombardment. Cover was
inadequate, and the Battalion suffered severely,
but digging was commenced at once and the line
taken up was rendered tenable.

Captain and Adjutant H. B. W. Maling was
dangerously wounded, and Major H. J. Nolan-
Ferrall was soon afterwards wounded in the
shoulder. Sergt.-Major Hudson, who had gone
out to the attack with C Company and had taken
part in the charge, was wounded in the leg, and
the streams of wounded men who were carried
or walked down to the dressing-station bore
testimony to the severity of the conflict.

Lieuts. J. E. Burke and Bennett had gallantly
laid down their lives, and Captains F. C. Burke,
B. W. Bond, and Lieuts. O. M. Tweedy, F. J.
Charlton, E. J. G. Kelly, T. W. G. Johnson, and
A. S. J. Mahony had all been wounded in gallantly
leading on their men. Ammunition was at once
brought up and distributed to all, and the Turkish
corpses were removed from the Sunken Road,
and this was made defensible at once. The
bombardment by the enemy's guns, however,
grew very heavy and caused many casualties.

The 5th Ghurkhas began to arrive at 5.15 p.m.,
and took up a position on the left of the Rangers
along the Sunken Road. They were, however,
unable to advance farther. D Company were
holding a farm-house about half a mile south of
Susak Kuyu, which was being subjected to heavy

machine-gun and rifle fire from the enemy. They were ordered to hand over their line to the 29th Indian Brigade, and rejoined headquarters near the well as soon as possible. The Company of the South Wales Borderers, which had issued from their lines after the trenches were taken, had begun to dig a trench between the Turkish trench and the Sunken Road; this was at once seen to be useless, as no field of fire could be obtained in any direction. As these troops were not under the command of Lieut.-Colonel H. F. N. Jourdain, the work was allowed to proceed, until the enemy began to concentrate his artillery on this trench, when it was discontinued.

All men available were now collected and at once organized to resist, if necessary, any counter-attack. The willingness with which all ranks worked both at the consolidation of the work and the position was admirable and beyond all praise. The barrier in the communication trench was now removed, and Lieut. A. J. W. Blake, with two platoons of A and B Companies, made his way up the trench and joined up with Brig.-General Russell's New Zealanders, who had seized a trench on the Kaiajik Aghala.

At 7.20 p.m. the Battalion, with the exception of some few men of D Company under Captain Webber, was concentrated, and all wounded men had been sent down to the dressing-station. An order had been sent out requesting Lieut.-Colonel Jourdain to advance up the slopes of the Kaiajik Aghala towards the Turkish trenches, but this was found impracticable, as the total strength of men then available for this operation was only forty. This attack was, however, attempted early next morning by the whole 18th Australian Battalion, but without success. The platoons of A and B under Lieut. Blake entered the New Zealand trenches, and behaved with great gallantry that night, during which Lieut. Blake was killed and also many of the splendid men he led so well. During these operations Sergeant Nealon was brought to notice for very gallant conduct. Communication was established with General Russell's New Zealanders soon after 7 p.m., and as orders now arrived for the Indian Brigade to take over the left of the position won, all the men of the Battalion were withdrawn from the Sunken Road and, with the exception of the machine-gun section, were ordered to the right, where a sap had commenced to be cut between the top of the communication trench and the trench occupied by the New Zealanders.

The line occupied by the Battalion was now divided into two sections, the right mainly com-posed of A and B Companies and near the New Zealand trench under Major Money, and the left with the men of C and D Companies and the machine-gun, which was located near the Well under Lieut.-Colonel Jourdain, the Commanding Officer. All the wounded had been safely evacuated; ammunition, bombs, and rations had been brought up, chiefly through the exertions of Captain R. J. H. Shaw and Lieut. R. R. Martin; water had been issued to all, and in addition rations and water had been brought up the communication trench

Map. No. II

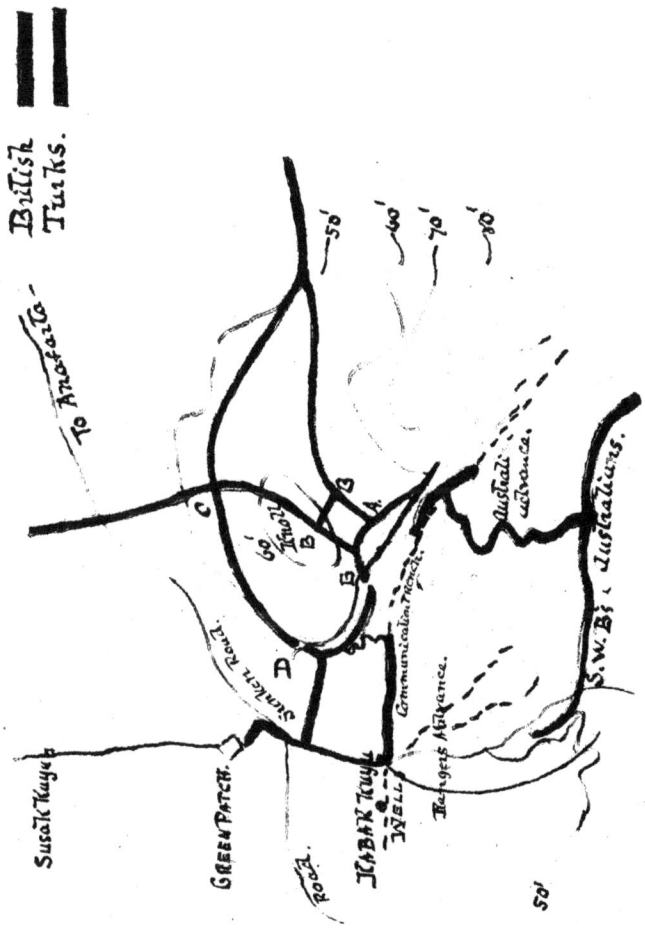

Positions of British and Turkish Lines on evening of 21st August 1915.
from a sketch by Major Mury D.S.O.

British
Turks.

N
S

Susak Kuyu
To Anofarta
Sunken Road
GREEN PATCH.
Road.
KABAK TUYU
WELL
C
B
A
Communication Trench.
Rangers Advance.
Australian Advance.
S.W.Bs.
Australians.
50'
50'
60'
70'
80'

and had been taken into the trenches occupied
by General Russell's New Zealanders. No details
of the defence were forgotten, and nothing was left
to chance. The men, encouraged by the spirit
of their officers, worked on without pause throughout the night, and the line was made quite secure
long before daylight dawned. By the swiftness
and unhesitating impulse of their charge the
Rangers had rushed the trenches before almost
the enemy had been aware of their advance, and
afterwards by dint of steadfastness and good work
the position had been made secure before any
counter-attack could be launched. The task was
accomplished, and the line had been extended
even beyond the desired limits.

The gallant officers and men, chiefly of A, C, and
D Companies, who, acting on the instructions to
help General Russell's attack if possible, advanced
beyond the Sunken Road up the slopes of the
Kaiajik Aghala and beyond the Green Patch,
were mown down by the hostile machine-gun
fire, and when afterwards the Turkish trenches
were captured, the dead could be seen extended
as at drill, each man facing towards the enemy.

Two officers and 89 men were afterwards buried
near the above-named places, while farther up
on the Kaiajik Aghala many more were ranged,
each man lying with his face towards the enemy,
and his rifle close beside him, showing that he
had used it to the last.

General Godley sent the following message to
the Battalion :—

' Delighted to hear your success ; stick fast to

what you have got, and congratulate the Connaught Rangers on their fine assault.'

A party of Australian soldiers, who had been sent to England wounded, were visiting the House of Commons on the 3rd November, 1915, and were introduced to Mr. John Redmond, M.P. Learning that they had been engaged in the battles in the Peninsula, Mr. Redmond inquired whether they had seen anything of the 10th Irish Division. They replied that indeed they had, for a portion of the 10th was attached to their division for a time, and they went on to express the highest admiration for the fighting qualities of the Irish soldiers. One charge by the Connaught Rangers was, they said, the finest thing they had seen in the war. This episode referred to the attack by the Rangers on the Turkish entrenchments near the wells at Kabak Kuyu.

On the 23rd August Lieut.-General Sir W. R. Birdwood, Major-General Sir A. Godley, and Major-General Sir H. V. Cox visited the Battalion, and expressed to Lieut.-Colonel Jourdain their highest approbation of the gallantry and prowess of the Battalion in the two previous days' actions.

At 10.10 p.m. on the 21st August, Brig.-General Russell, under whose orders the Battalion had been placed at 6.40 p.m. that evening, visited the Battalion in the trenches and informed the Commanding Officer that the Rangers were to attack again in the morning, and that the sap to the New Zealand trenches should be finished that night if possible.

All men not on the look-out were employed all night at trench work. Soon after midnight on the night of 21st–22nd August at 12.20 a.m., the Turks assembled in large masses and made their way up to the trenches manned by the New Zealanders and other Regiments. They did not open fire, however, but attempted to rush the trenches by feigning surrender.

This attack was beaten off, but not before it began to assume a formidable aspect. At 5.15 a.m. on the same date (22nd August) the enemy made a second attack, and creeping up through the low scrub, suddenly broke into loud cries of ' Allah ! Allah ! ' and tried to storm the trenches on the Kaiajik Aghala. The attack was, however, again beaten off by rifle fire and bombs, and the whole position won remained in the hands of the British. The hostile snipers occasionally crept up to the lines and attempted to pick off any one who might be unwary, and one Turk was wounded and actually brought in by a picquet of the Rangers as a prisoner, only a few yards from the line.

At 10.30 a.m. A Company was sent in to the Battalion bivouac of the 20th August. The enemy continued to shell the trenches held by the Rangers during the day of the 22nd August, and there were several casualties.

Many of the men, who had worked ceaselessly throughout the night, when relieved from duty on the 22nd August, at once fell asleep, and slept soundly. The 18th Battalion Australian Infantry were brought up and attacked the Turkish trenches on the morning of the 22nd August, which they took, but were in their turn counter-attacked and driven out.

There were now left only seven officers of the Battalion, of whom Lieuts. Lewis and Godber had been employed under the Brigade Commander on the previous day. The other officers remaining were :—

Lieut.-Colonel H. F. N. Jourdain (commanding).
Major N. C. K. Money.
Captain A. Webber.
Lieut. R. R. Martin.
2nd Lieut. C. F. B. Harvey,

the last of whom accompanied A Company into camp at 10.30 a.m.

The day wore on, and towards evening came the welcome news that the Battalion would be relieved from trench duty that evening, and would return to their bivouac of the 20th, leaving 50 men under an officer at Kabak Kuyu Well, which had been surrounded by a bullet-proof wall of sandbags, making the passage of troops up the communication trench and the Sunken Road quite secure.

The day of the 22nd had been insufferably hot, and the hard work of the last two days had taxed the strength even of the strongest. The gallantry and bearing of all ranks had been above all praise, and the devotion to duty of Lieut. O'Sullivan, R.A.M.C., at the dressing-station had enabled all those wounded to be conveyed, after their wounds had been dressed, to the beach to await the arrival of the next hospital ship.

The stretcher-bearers, as usual, acquitted themselves excellently, as did also the signallers under Sergt. Gaugheran. Lieut. A. J. W. Blake, who was killed in action in the New Zealand trench, was buried in the trench that night by the men with whom he had fought, and among whom he had gallantly laid down his life. A platoon and a half under this officer fought throughout the night with the New Zealanders, and acquitted themselves most gallantly. The closing part of the narrative, as furnished by the Commanding Officer to Brigade Headquarters, is here quoted in detail:—

'I cannot too much praise the fortitude under fire and the good work of the officers, N.C.O.s and men of the Battalion under my command, and I shall have pleasure in bringing to notice later the names of those whom I have selected for forwarding to the Brigadier.

'I would like to mention that great personal bravery was shown by 2nd Lieut. T. W. G. Johnson, whose name has been already forwarded, and great dash was shown by Captain F. C. Burke, Captain B. W. Bond, 2nd Lieut. J. E. Burke, Lieut. A. J. W. Blake, and 2nd Lieut. G. R. Bennett, and I derived much assistance from Major N. C. K. Money, who was the only senior officer left to assist me at 5.20 p.m. on the 21st August. The movements of the leading companies were done with a precision which was admirable, and the behaviour of all ranks was beyond praise. There were many Turkish dead on the field, comprising nearly 100 dead in the vicinity of Kabak Kuyu and along the continuation of the Sunken Road, and one German officer, who was wearing blue gorget patches.

'There were also more than 200 dead in front of the right end of the New Zealand trenches, and more than a hundred between the left of the New Zealand trenches and the right of the trenches of the 5th Ghurkhas, which had been taken by the Rangers. I am also glad to say that some platoons of the Rangers fought in the New Zealand trenches on the night of the 21st–22nd August, and behaved admirably.'

On the 30th August the following names were submitted to the Brigadier for those officers and non-commissioned officers and men who had distinguished themselves in the presence of the enemy on the dates mentioned against their names :—

Major N. C. K. Money (Captain 22nd Punjabis), for gallantry on the 21st and 22nd August and for continued good service near Kabak Kuyu.

Captain and Adjutant H. B. W. Maling, for gallantry in delivering a message under fire on the 21st August at Kabak Kuyu and for good service. (Severely wounded.)

Lieut. A. J. W. Blake (killed in action). For great gallantry in command of a detachment of the 5th Battalion the Connaught Rangers, when holding a trench captured from the Turks on the 21st August near Kabak Kuyu. This officer was killed on this duty. He had kept the enemy at bay for several hours before he was killed, and had shown great gallantry.

2nd Lieut. T. W. G. Johnson. This officer's 1915 services have already been sent forward for special mention. After gallantly leading his platoon, he entered a trench and bayoneted six Turks with his own bayonet, afterwards shooting two more. (Severely wounded.)

No. 5/642, Sergt. John O'Connell, on the 22nd August went out most gallantly under a heavy fire and brought in a wounded New Zealander, who was endeavouring to reach safety, but was unable to do so. Also for gallant conduct on the 21st and 22nd August at Kabak Kuyu. Has shown conspicuous gallantry throughout.

No. 5/319, Sergt. M. Nealon, on the night of the 21st–22nd August, held the right end of the New Zealand trench with a few men with great gallantry. Barricaded and held the Turkish communication trench during the afternoon and evening of the 21st August. After the officer commanding the party had been killed on the night of the 21st August, Sergt. Nealon took command and gallantly fought on throughout the night.

No. 6757, Sergt. John McIlwain. For gallantry on the 21st August ; after his platoon commander had been wounded took command and advanced his platoon against the Turkish trenches at Kabak Kuyu, and afterwards in the advance on Susak Kuyu. After his Company had been relieved, Sergt. McIlwain received permission to remain

1915 behind and bring in the wounded, which he did with the utmost gallantry. A Sergeant and one man who had been told off for this purpose had both been killed. This N.C.O. acted throughout with the greatest gallantry and encouraged the men by his brave conduct.

No. 5/824, Corporal J. Doyle, gave great assistance to Sergt. Nealon in defending his trench on the morning of the 22nd August, until he was wounded.

A special order by General Sir Ian Hamilton, G.C.B., D.S.O., A.D.C., is given in detail :—

SPECIAL ORDER

By

GENERAL SIR IAN HAMILTON, G.C.B., D.S.O., A.D.C., Commander-in-Chief, Mediterranean Expeditionary Force.

GENERAL HEADQUARTERS,

Mediterranean Expeditionary Force.

7th September, 1915.

The Commander-in-Chief, Mediterranean Expeditionary Force, desires formally to record the fine feat of arms achieved by the troops under the command of Lieutenant-General Sir W. R. Birdwood during the battle of Sari Bair.

The fervent desire of all ranks to close with the enemy, the impetuosity of their onset and the steadfast valour with which they maintained the long struggle, these will surely make appeal to their fellow-countrymen all over the world.

The gallant capture of the almost impregnable Lone Pine trenches by the Australian Division, and the equally gallant defence of the position against repeated counter-attacks, are exploits which will live in history. The determined assaults carried out from other parts of the Australian Division's line were also of inestimable service to the whole force, preventing as they did the movement of large bodies of reinforcements to the northern flank.

The troops under the command of Major-General Sir A. J. Godley, and particularly the New Zealand and Australian Division, were called upon to carry out one of the most difficult military operations that has ever been attempted—a night march and assault by several columns in intricate mountainous country, strongly entrenched, and held by a numerous and determined enemy. Their brilliant conduct during this operation and the success they achieved have won for them a reputation as soldiers of whom any country must be proud.

To the Australian and New Zealand Army Corps, therefore, and to those who were associated with that famous Corps in the battle of Sari Bair— the Maoris, Sikhs, Gurkhas, and the new troops of the 10th and 13th Divisions from the Old Country —Sir Ian Hamilton tenders his appreciation of their efforts, his admiration of their gallantry, and his thanks for their achievements. It is an honour to command a force which numbers such men as these in its ranks, and it is the Commander-in-Chief's high privilege to acknowledge that honour.

(Sd.)   W. P. BRAITHWAITE,

Major-General,

Chief of the General Staff.

General Sir Ian Hamilton, in his report on the operations, states :—

' On the 21st August we had carried the Turkish entrenchments at several points, but had been unable to hold what we had gained except along the section where Major-General Cox had made a good advance with Anzac and Indian troops.'

The Battalion was highly complimented by the Officer Commanding the 5th Ghurkha Rifles—a most gallant and brave officer—on the dash and bravery shown by the Regiment in their attack on the Turkish position.

The losses in the Battalion up to the 20th August, 1915, were :—

Officers: wounded 6		
sick 1		
	—	7
Other Ranks: killed . . . 15		
wounded . . . 120		
sick 78		
	—	213
Casualties, total all ranks . . .		220

The losses in the Battalion during the two days' fighting (the 21st and 22nd August) were as follows :—

Total. 1915

Officers killed : Lieut. Blake, 2nd Lieuts.
    J. E. Burke and G. R. Bennett . . . 3

Officers wounded : Major Nolan - Ferrall,
    Captain F. C. Burke, Captain and
    Adjutant H. B. W. Maling, Captain
    B. W. Bond, Lieut. O. M. Tweedy,
    Lieut. F. J. Charlton, 2nd Lieut. A. St. J.
    Mahony, 2nd Lieut. E. J. G. Kelly,
    and 2nd Lieut. T. W. G. Johnson .   9

Warrant Officers : Sergt.-Major J. Hudson   1

Killed, other ranks : A, 9 ; B, 6 ; C, 11 ;
    D, 17 43

Wounded, other ranks : A, 30 ; B, 34 ; C, 46 ;
    D, 48 158

Missing, other ranks : A, 11 ; B, 2 ; C, 20 ;
    D, 14 47

All ranks, total 261

The numbers of killed and wounded up to
    the 20th August had been . . . 141

The total number of men sent sick up to date
    had been 85

Total casualties up to 22nd August 487

The hostile rifle and gun fire slackened very
much during the afternoon of the 22nd August,
and almost died away towards evening. The
orders were for the 18th Battalion Australian
Infantry to relieve the 5th Battalion Connaught
Rangers soon after 5 p.m. the same evening. This
was the same Battalion which had come up in the

F

early morning and which had made a gallant effort to take the trenches on Hill 60, which task had at first been assigned to the 5th Battalion by Brig. General Russell on the evening of the 21st August.

A few details deserve to be narrated, and one of these was the gallant defence of a small trench by about 30 men of the Rangers, of whom only two returned alive the next morning ; also in another small trench, which had been seized by three men on the afternoon of the 21st, and was actually held until they had been ordered to evacuate it by the Officer Commanding the 5th Ghurkhas, as the trench was of no real use and quite untenable. These men made a splendid defence, two being wounded. The pioneers of the Battalion had named the two wells ' Rangers Well '—No. 1 and No. 2, and boards were affixed to them with the names neatly carved on them. Some few days afterwards these boards were removed, and in the official dispatch the capture of the wells was at first attributed to the Indian Brigade.

Captain Pollok, the Brigade-Major of the Brigade, had been wounded near the New Zealand trench early in the afternoon, but did not wish to be moved until evening ; however, two men of the Battalion went out at 4.15 p.m., and under a heavy fire brought in Captain Pollok in a most brave and gallant fashion, which was commended by the Commanding Officer.

The capture of the wells was afterwards referred to Lieut.-General Sir Alexander Godley, and the correspondence referred to will be found at the end of the narrative.

At 7.20 p.m. on the 22nd August Lieut.-Colonel Jourdain led the way out of the trenches and marched the Battalion back to the bivouac in what was called 'South Wales Borderers' Gully', and where the Quartermaster had tea ready for those who returned.

As the Battalion wended its way back to the bivouac of two nights ago, in the fast fading light, the traces of the fight of that afternoon were still apparent, and many dead Turks lay about and in the bushes by the dusty track. Rifles and equipment belonging to the enemy were everywhere, and traces of the deadly combat were to be seen in every trench and even across the open ground, where the men of C and D Companies had debouched into the open with the ancient yell of Connaught on their lips. The bivouac was reached at 7.45 p.m., and the roll was called. The total strength of the Battalion now was :—

Seven officers	7
and 402 other ranks	402
Total	409

These numbers included all men, whether employed with Quartermaster's Department or with Brigade Headquarters.

The work and strain for the past 27 hours had been very great, and soon after the arrival of the Battalion in their camp, both officers and men were sound asleep.

At 11.15 a.m. on the 23rd August Lieut.-General Sir W. R. Birdwood, Major-General Sir A. Godley, and Major-General Cox, C.B., C.S.I., arrived up

from Anzac, and asked to see Lieut.-Colonel Jourdain.   General Sir W. R. Birdwood said he came
to congratulate the Battalion, and wished to say
how splendidly the Rangers had done.   He called
for any special cases of gallantry, and before leaving repeated the assurance that the Battalion had
done really well.   General Sir Alexander Godley
also congratulated the Battalion, and said how glad
he was they had done so well.   The Commanding
Officer reported the gallantry of 2nd Lieut. Johnson, and General Sir W. R. Birdwood promised to
exert his influence to get him a Military Cross.

To the Commanding Officer General Birdwood
said he was very much indebted to the Rangers, and
promised that the Battalion should have four days'
rest, when he knew they would be ready for more
work again.   General Cox also tendered his congratulations, as did Lieut.-Colonel Agnew, who
visited the Battalion later.

Subsequently the Rangers were ordered to send
100 men under an officer, on inlying picquet behind
the lines of the South Wales Borderers, and to hold
fifty more in readiness for any emergency.   During
the night there was a most violent discharge of
musketry, otherwise the night passed quietly.
One man was wounded to-day (23rd August).

On the 24th August the Rangers remained in
bivouac near the Damakjelik Bair, but provided
parties to bring up ammunition and supports for
the firing line.

The enemy expended a vast amount of ammunition and bombs against the trench line the previous
night, and sleep was almost out of the question until

the firing died away. On the next day (25th August)
British aeroplanes announced that Turkish reinforcements were arriving in numbers on the left
of the trenches in the front of the Battalion. The
Fifth accordingly provided again a strong inlying
picquet this day and throughout the night.

On the 26th August forty men were sent in to
Shrapnel Gully to obtain as many of the great-coats
and kits of the Battalion, which had been there
since August 6th.

During the afternoon the Turkish gunners shelled
the bivouac, and wounded one man of the Rangers
and one Australian. Some rain fell that night, and
again in the evening, and the arrival of the officers'
valises and great-coats for the men was very much
appreciated.

A picquet of fifty men, under Captain Webber,
was sent up to the supporting lines the same night.

The 25th August had been the first day since
the 5th August, when the Battalion landed on the
Peninsula, that there had been no casualty in the
Regiment. One man was wounded, however, on
the 26th August.

The Commanding Officer and Major Money proceeded to the headquarters of Major-General Cox
at 4.45 p.m. on the 26th August, to receive orders
as to the concerted action which was to be taken
against the Turkish position on the Kaiajik Aghala
on the next day.   The dash of the Battalion on the
21st August was praised by all the Generals present
at the conference.

Early on the 27th August the two chaplains of
the Brigade—the Rev. T. J. O'Connor, Roman

1915 Catholic Chaplain, and the Rev. J. W. Crozier, Church of England Chaplain—celebrated Divine Service for the men of the Battalion.

The Brigadier, with Lieut.-Colonel Jourdain and Major Money, proceeded up to the advanced trenches and viewed the Turkish position and the trenches the Rangers were to be called upon to take the same afternoon. The men of the Battalion were to advance to their position at 2.30 p.m. and to be in position at 3 p.m.

The artillery bombardment was to begin at 4 p.m. and to end at 5 p.m., with a pause of five minutes from 4.30 p.m. to 4.35 p.m. The assaulting column was composed of 250 men, under Major Money and Lieut. S. H. Lewis, nearly all volunteers and selected men from A, B, and C Companies.

These men were organized in four parties of twenty-five men each, and three of fifty each, so that each party should push forward under its own officer or N.C.O., regardless of the others.

The remainder of the Battalion was placed under Captain A. Webber as a general reserve.

There were, however, only forty-four men in this reserve, several of whom were even then suffering from severe attacks of dysentery. The route to the trenches over which the Battalion had attacked on the 21st was now connected by a deep and splendidly made sap or communication trench. The duties of all were carefully explained both by the Commanding Officer and by the officers commanding the storming parties, and every man knew his duties and the part he had to play. All men carried two sandbags, and 40 per cent. also

had either pick or shovel in addition to their arms. 1915
220 rounds per man was also carried.

The operation order by Major-General Cox is
given in detail here :—

OPERATION ORDER NO. I, BY MAJOR-GENERAL COX,
   C.B., C.S.I., COMMANDING NO. 6 SECTION SARI
   BAIR ATTACKING FORCE.

26th August, 1915.

I.   Under orders from G.O.C. N.Z.A. Division
operations will be undertaken commencing at
16 hours to-morrow (4 p.m.) (27th August) with
the object of gaining commanding ground on the
Kaiajik Aghala Hill.

II.   (1) The objectives are as marked on the
accompanying sketch A to B, viz. Turkish trenches
in front of the 4th Australian detachment.

(2) B to C, viz. long Turkish communication
trench running over Hill 60.

(3) C to D, a line of Turkish trench from the
communicating trench on Knoll 60 round north of
hill to present left of New Zealand trench on
Kaiajik Aghala.

III.   The following artillery co-operation and
previous bombardment has been arranged for, the
latter to operate at 16 hours on 27th.

(a) *Naval guns* on enemy's trenches on Asma
Dere spur, also on Abdel Rahman Bair, and on
valley beyond Kaiajik Aghala, till dark.

(b) *Howitzers*, &c., commencing at 16 hours 27th
on Knoll 60, Kaiajik Aghala and enemy's trenches
on it, east of a line 92–I–J and 92–N–O–1–4, steady

rate of fire 16 hours to 16.30, 5 minutes break and intense fire 16.35 to 17 hours. During above period some fire on NE. spur of Kaiajik Dere from Kaiajik Aghala to knoll at contour 100 inclusive. After assault (17 hours) steady fire on NE. spur Kaiajik Dere as described above till dark, and to search low ground beyond the spur.

(c) *Field Artillery*, generally the valley between Dervish Ali Kuyu and Kaiajik Aghala and roads by which reinforcements from east must move up—16 hours till dark—intense fire on spur NE. of Kaiajik Dere from 16–35 to 17 hours.

(d) *Mountain Artillery*, as for Field Artillery—also 2 guns 21st Mountain Battery at close range on to hostile Kaiajik Aghala trenches from the main trenches held by the 4th Australian Brigade.

N.B.—Day's registration to be over by 12 noon.

IV. To assist the artillery it is of the *utmost importance* that the trenches we now hold on the Kaiajik Aghala shall be marked by red or pink flags at 15 hours, to be placed so as not to be seen by the enemy, also that the trenches gained shall be marked by other red flags as occupied. Flags have been arranged for. During the preliminary bombardment all infantry in advanced trenches (except a few look-out men in secure spots) will sit down at bottom of their trenches with their backs to the parapet.

V. The [following force is detailed for the assault on the objectives named in paragraph 2 of this order :—

Right, viz.—to capture trenches A–B (on 1915 sketch).

250 4th Australian Brigade.

100 17th Battalion 5th Australian Brigade.

Centre—to capture trenches B–C.

300 New Zealand Mounted Rifles Brigade.

100 18th Battalion, 5th Australian Brigade.

Left—to capture trench C–D.

250 men Connaught Rangers, 29th Infantry Brigade.

Detailed orders will be issued to each of the above parties by Brig.-General Russell, who is placed in command of the assaulting force and will arrange for consolidating and linking up new line when gained.

VI.   *The Assault* will take place at 17 hours on 27th precisely.   Watches to be compared at Brigade Headquarters, No. 6 Section, at 10 hours on 27th.

VII.   All infantry going forward will carry 220 rounds, and two empty sandbags per man, and each party will have bombers specially detailed and well supplied with bombs.

Attacking troops must have one day's rations and full water-bottles with them.   Entrenching tools will be carried by 40 per cent. of the attacking force.

A forward reserve of S.A.A. ammunition of 50 rounds per man for the attacking force will be formed close behind our present trenches on Kaiajik Aghala.

1915   VIII. Reserves will be held in readiness if
required, as follows :—

(*a*) In gully near new communicating trench to
Kaiajik Aghala (outside our former line), from
4th Australian Brigade trenches.

100 men { 50 from 4th Australian Brigade.
          50 from 17th Battalion, 5th Australian
               Brigade.

(*b*) At Kabak Kuyu—100 men, 18th Battalion,
5th Australian Brigade.

To be fully equipped as in preceding paragraph.

IX. *Medical.*—First aid posts, first field dress-
ing-stations, stand fast in present positions.

X. Telephonic reports for G.O.C. No. 6 Section,
to headquarters, 4th Australian Brigade. Reports
by hand to trenches, 13th Battalion, 4th Australian
Brigade.

Both after 14.30 hours on 27th.

(Sd.) G. W. PEPYS, Captain,

Brigade-Major, No. 6 Section.

To Brig.-General Russell—2 copies.
To Brig.-General Monash—2 copies.
Colonel Agnew, 29th Brigade—2 copies.
N.Z.A. Division—1 copy.
Colonel Napier-Johnston—1 copy.
C.R.A., N.Z.A. Division—2 copies.
Colonel Sykes, R.A.—1 copy.
Colonel Parker, O.C.M.A. Brigade—1 copy.
O.C. 21st Kohat M.B.—1 copy.
Office—1 copy.

The officer commanding the attacking force

wished all the assaulting forces to be in position
at 3 p.m. It was, however, some minutes past
that hour before the Rangers got up to their
assigned position, as the trenches by which they
made their way up to the advanced trenches
were not wide and hardly able to contain their
dusky occupants ; and meanwhile the enemy
kept up an accurate fire on any one who showed
himself. Lieut.-Colonel Jourdain reported all
parties in position before the bombardment began,
and all troops then were ordered to sit close, in
case they might be hit by splinters which accompanied the bombardment. Punctually at 4 p.m.
the concentrated bombardment began, and the
noise was simply terrific, many of the shells burst-
ing on the Kaiajik Aghala, and covering even the
men in the trenches with dust and stones, so close
were the explosions, but still the accuracy of the
artillery was wonderful. At 5 p.m. the bombardment ceased, and the storming party of the
Rangers, led by Lieut. Lewis, leapt over the
parapet and charged forward to the Turkish trench.
More men began to climb over ; but the enemy,
who had got the exact range of the parapet whence
the assaulting party of the Rangers emerged into
the open, now opened with shrapnel, machine-gun
fire, and rifle fire. Whole sections were simply
carried away by the extraordinary outburst of the
enemy's fire, and the trench was choked with the
headless, bleeding, and torn fragments of the
brave sons of Ireland, who had but a few minutes
before pushed forward with such spirit and
determination. The first 50 men had got over

1915 and made their way at once down the Turkish trench, although greatly obstructed by the large numbers of Turkish dead which lay in the trench, the victims of the British bombardment.

As more men mounted the parapet the enemy's fire became intense and was concentrated on the trenches occupied by the Connaught Rangers, and caused heavy loss, the whole parapet being blown in by their high explosive shells. The second line of the 5th Battalion made their way up on either side of the Turkish trench, many of the enemy being bayoneted among the low scrub. Before many minutes another line was thrown forward, and meeting some of the New Zealanders lay down for a brief space of time, and then all rushed forward together and made directly for point C. This line did not make a continuous rush, but lay down once to avoid the cross-fire that assailed them. The leading party, making short work of the occupants of the trench, reached the point C, and were soon after joined by the other parties before 5.30 p.m.

The fourth party was now sent forward, which made its way across the open, but losing heavily, occupied the trenches near point C.

During this time a bombing party of nine men worked its way up from D to C, but was much hampered by the piles of Turkish dead and débris in the trenches. In some places the dead were even six deep, and never were there less than two deep along the whole trench from D to C.

The Rangers in occupation of Point C signalled back to the Ghurkha observation post that the whole trench was occupied at 5.57 p.m. Of the storming party of 250 men, nearly half had fallen. Lieut. Lewis, wounded in the knee and elbow, had reached the end of the trench, but was unwilling to retrace his steps, wounded though he was, even to have his wounds dressed.

When the Turks commenced to counter-attack it became impossible to communicate with him, and he was seen no more. Of a truly brave and chivalrous nature he refused to be taken back, in order that some of his men whom he led so well might be succoured.

When, afterwards, volunteers were called for to search for him, numbers of men went boldly out, but without success. The trench was, however, swept by the Rangers, and although they had to face a very severe cross-fire both from guns and machine-guns, the men never faltered, but went gallantly on with a swiftness and cohesion that drew forth general acclamation. The lines were mown down by the enemy's deadly fire, but the task was completed, and the trench was held and manned by the Rangers with a few New Zealanders who had made their way across to Point C, with their comrades of the 5th Battalion of the Connaught Rangers.

On the north side of this trench there were two approaches or communication trenches which were then unknown to the Staff of the Australian and New Zealand Army Corps, while on the southern side was a long trench which communicated with the trench B–C, near the Point B. The existence of these trenches was unknown, but was very detrimental to the defence. The reserve, under Captain A. Webber, was ordered up at a few minutes to 6 p.m., but was not at once pushed up the Turkish trench. The enemy now began to make their way up from the two trenches on the north side, and after some stiff fighting cut off and killed those who were holding the trench near Point C, at 10.29 p.m.

The right column, which had been checked by machine-gun fire, could make no headway.

The trench won by the Rangers was soon attacked by nearly 2,000 of the enemy, who had now been hurried up. At 12.25 a.m. only the upper part of the trench had been won back by the Turks, but over 150 men had fallen, and Major Money reported that he could not hold on longer without support. The only reserve available (44 men under Captain Webber) had been sent up the Turkish trench, but Captain Webber had been wounded and several men, and the hordes of Turkish bombers pressing on compelled the few remaining defenders to fall back towards D. Here, however, they made a stand and effectually beat off all attacks made on them. The 9th Australian Light Horse were now brought up, and attempted to retake the part of the trench which had been given up, at 3.45 a.m. on the 28th August, but were unable to do so. The trench was now barricaded by Major Money and made secure, and measures were taken to consolidate the new line. As the part of the trench held by the Rangers at and beyond Point D was too crowded, and there was no immediate prospect of another advance that day, some of the men, 32 in number, were withdrawn by the Commanding Officer before 4 a.m., and these fell back to the Headquarters near the 5th Ghurkhas' trenches.

The Turks advanced down the communication trenches to the north of the trench D to C, which the troops on Chocolate Hill had seen them digging since the 21st August, fearing no doubt that they would be attacked before long, and making ingress or egress to their line quite easy. The Turkish main trench from D to C was, however, dug in the shape of a V, and very soon became quite choked with the dead and the débris from the bombardment, beams, stones, &c. When the storming party attempted to make their way along this, they found progress almost impossible, and even when the trench was again captured on the night of the 28th–29th August, it took several days to remove the many Turkish corpses which absolutely barred the passage along the trench. Very heavy loss was inflicted on the Turks, and many were bayoneted by the Rangers in their impetuous dash towards Point C on the sketch.

Major-General Cox sent the following message :—

' Send my heartiest congratulations to all ranks ; am reporting their gallantry to the Division. Tell them to hold on tight. Meantime hold on and accept my congratulations of the great gallantry of your Regiment.'

Major-General Sir A. Godley wired :—

' Heartiest congratulations from the New Zealand and Australian Division on your brilliant achievement this evening, which is a fitting sequel to the capture of Kabak Kuyu Well and will go down to history among the finest feats of your distinguished Regiment. Personally, as an Irishman who has served in two Irish Regiments, it gives me the greatest pride and pleasure that the Regiment should have performed such gallant deeds under my command. Stick to what you have got and consolidate.'

The official attack on Knoll 60 is also given here :—

ATTACK ON KNOLL 60, 27th, 28th, 29th AUGUST.

September 3rd, 1915.

' During the action of 21st August a footing had been gained on Knoll 60 north of Kaiajik Aghala, but the knoll itself had not been captured. The capture of the hill was entrusted to Major-General Cox. The bombardment commenced at 4 p.m. and was continued until 5 p.m., at which hour the assault was delivered, on the right by 350 rifles from the 4th and 5th Australian Brigades, in the centre by 400 rifles of the New Zealand Mounted Rifles and 5th Australian Brigade, and on the left by 250 rifles of the 5th Bn. Connaught Rangers. The attack instantly drew a heavy fire of enemy's shrapnel, machine-guns and rifles, followed shortly afterwards by heavy shell on the knoll and shrapnel all over the position, including trenches still occupied by the Turks. The Connaught Rangers, showing brilliant dash in attack, reached their objective and commenced a gallant fight along the communication trench.

MAP. No. III.

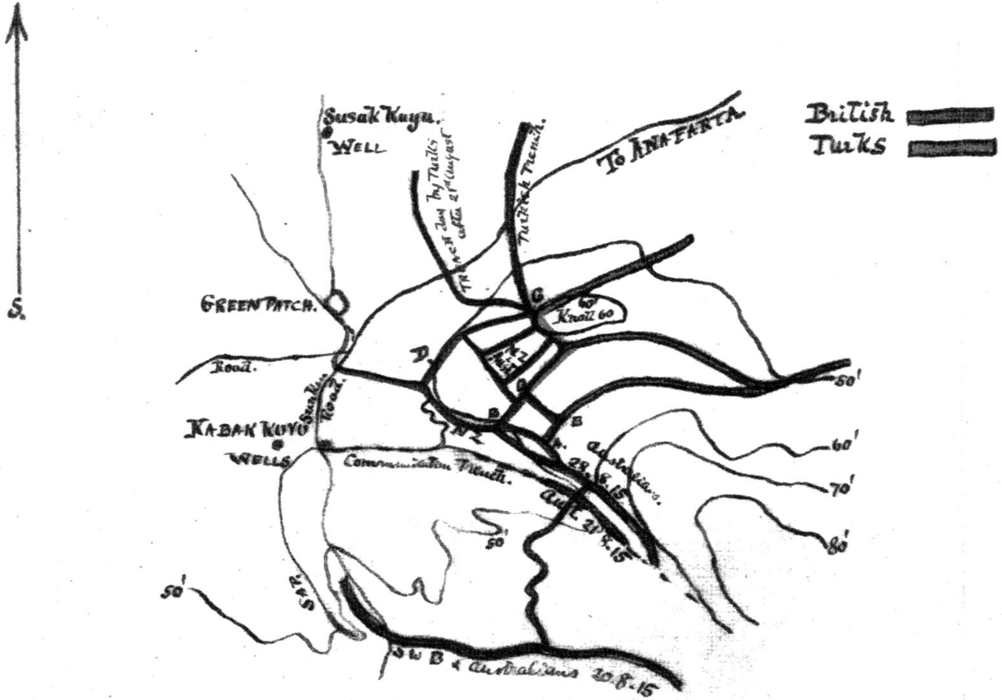

N ← → S.

British ▬▬▬▬
Turks ▬▬▬▬

To ANAFARTA

Susak Kuyu
WELL

GREEN PATCH.

Road.

KABAK KUYU
WELLS

Knoll 60

Turkish Trench.

Trenches held by Turks
after attack of 27 August

Kaba Tepe
Road.

Communication Trench.

Australians.

8th B & Australians 26.8.15

50'
60'
70'
80'

50'

S.A.R.

Position of British and Turks on August 29th 1915, after attacks of 27th and 28th August 1915,
from a sketch by Major Money I.S.O.
Aug. 1915.

Atkinson Lieut.-Colonel
's The Commanding 1st Regiment.

The right column was, however, checked by 1915 machine-gun fire, and for some time could make no headway. In the centre the New Zealanders, with splendid dash, carried the cross-communication trench, but were held up before reaching the top of the knoll, and confused fighting continued till 9.30 p.m., by which time about nine-tenths of the objective had been taken. It was arranged to put fresh troops in to capture the remainder of the hill at midnight. Before this could be done, however, the Connaught Rangers were bombed out of their position, and the 9th Australian Light Horse who attempted to retake it at 3.45 a.m. were unable to do so. During the 28th the day was spent in consolidating gains and making communication trenches from the original line, and preparations were made to take the remainder of the knoll on the night of the 28th–29th. At one o'clock on the morning of the 29th the 10th Australian Light Horse carried the trench on the top and retained it, and the knoll passed into our possession. The position has been consolidated, and a good view is now obtained over the valley to the North.

' This gallant action adds 400 more acres of Turkish territory to the country occupied by Anzac. The fighting during these operations was almost entirely hand-to-hand and of a very severe nature. The brunt of the fighting was borne by the Indian Brigade, the New Zealand Mounted Rifles Brigade, the 5th Battalion Connaught Rangers, the 4th Battalion South Wales Borderers, the 13th and 14th Battalions of the 4th Australian

G

Infantry Brigade, and the 18th Battalion of the 5th Australian Brigade. The 9th and 10th Australian Light Horse Regiments were also engaged and took a conspicuous part in the final assault, the posts of honour in the line of Turkish trenches which we eventually held being occupied by the New Zealand Mounted Rifle Brigade and the 10th Australian Light Horse, supported by a mixed detachment of the 4th Australian Infantry Brigade.

' The casualties in this force amounted to about 1,000 of all ranks, but very heavy loss was inflicted on the Turks, not only in the desperate hand-to-hand fighting in the trenches but also from the artillery bombardment.

' Three machine-guns, two of which were used at once against the Turks, and 46 prisoners were taken, as well as three trench mortars, 300 Turkish rifles, 60,000 rounds of small arm ammunition, and 500 bombs. Judging by the heaps of Turkish dead in the trenches, and observation from the Kaiajik Dere trenches, which commanded the Turkish line of retreat, and owing to our artillery getting at the Turks during the retreat, it is estimated that the Turkish losses must have been at least 5,000.'

It was a brilliant achievement, and one of which the other Battalions of the Regiment may be justly proud. It had been found necessary to include even the Company cooks in the attack on the 27th to make up the requisite numbers, and Private Glavey, who was even at enlistment somewhat past the military age, as he had three sons serving in France, when he heard Major Money ask who was next to get over the parapet, even in the teeth of a storm of shot and shell, answered gaily : ' I have three sons fighting in France, and one of them has won the D.C.M. Let's see if the old father cannot get one now.' He sprang to the top of the trench, but a shell struck him, and he did not return to answer the roll call.

Lance-Corporal MacNeely, too, deserves special mention, when with his bayonet dripping with blood, after having bayoneted six Turks, calmly inquired in the midst of a storm of machine-gun fire, if there were any more of the enemy about. He was then standing in the open, and the bullets were even then ripping up the ground on which he stood, and he was at that time unwounded. He also never returned to answer the call, and his bones now rest in the Peninsula beside those with whom he fought so well. There were many other instances of gallant and devoted conduct, which would be too numerous to mention. The losses of the storming party speak for themselves, two officers and 152 other ranks killed, wounded, and missing, truly a terrible toll for such a small force engaged.

The officers wounded were :—

Captain A. Webber (wounded).
Lieut. S. H. Lewis (wounded and missing, believed killed).

Of those that were missing it was known that the majority, if not all, had died at their posts in the advanced part of the trench, although outnumbered by thousands of Turks, who were brought up at once, when it was seen that our objective was to seize the enemy trenches on the Kaiajik Aghala.

The experiment of placing the men in parties of 50 and 25 under their special leaders, as these men had perforce to be drawn from all companies of the Battalion, worked exceedingly well, and although only three officers were available for this duty, the other parties were under the non-commissioned officers of their own companies whom they knew so well. Among these Sergt. John O'Connell deserves a place in the records of the Battalion as a splendid example to his men.

General Sir Ian Hamilton describes the operations of the 27th and 28th August in the following terms :—

' The last days of the month were illumined by a brilliant affair carried through by the troops under General Birdwood's command. Our object was to complete the capture of Hill 60 north of the Kaiajik Aghala, commenced by Major-General Cox on the 21st August. Hill 60 overlooked the Biyuk Anafarta valley, and was therefore tactically a very important feature.

' The conduct of the attack was again entrusted to Major-General Cox, at whose disposal were placed detachments from the 4th and 5th Australian Brigades, the New Zealand Mounted Rifles Brigade, and the 5th The Connaught Rangers.

' The advance was timed to take place at 5 p.m. on the 27th of August, after the heaviest artillery bombardment we could afford. This bombard-

ment seemed effective ; but the moment the
assailants broke cover they were greeted by an
exceedingly hot fire from the enemy field-guns,
rifles, and machine-guns, followed after a brief
interval by a shower of heavy shell, some of which,
most happily, pitched into the trenches of the
Turks.   On the right the detachment from the
4th and 5th Australian Brigades could make no
headway against a battery of machine-guns which
confronted them. In the centre the New Zealanders
made a most determined onslaught, and carried one
side of the topmost knoll.

'Hand-to-hand fighting continued here till 9.30
p.m., when it was reported that nine-tenths of the
summit had been gained.

' On the left the 250 men of the Connaught
Rangers excited the admiration of all beholders
by the swiftness and cohesion of their charge.   In
five minutes they had carried their objective, the
northern Turkish communications, when they at
once set to and began a lively bomb-fight along
the trenches against strong parties which came
hurrying up from the enemy supports and afterwards from their reserves.   At midnight fresh
troops were to have strengthened our grip upon the
hill, but before that hour the Irishmen had been
out-bombed, and the 9th Australian Light Horse,
who had made a most plucky attempt to recapture
the lost communication trench, had been repulsed.

' At 1 a.m. on the 29th August the 10th Light
Horse made another attack on the lost communication trenches to the left, carried them, and
finally held them. This gave us complete command

of the underfeature, an outlook over the Anafarta Sagir valley, and safer lateral communications between Anzac and Suvla Bay.

'Our casualties in this hotly contested affair amounted to 1,000. The Turks lost out of all proportion more. Their line of retreat was commanded from our Kaiajik Dere trenches, whence our observers were able to direct artillery fire equally upon their fugitives and their reinforcements. The same observers estimated the Turkish casualties as no less than 5,000. Three Turkish machine-guns and forty-six prisoners were taken, as well as three trench mortars, 300 Turkish rifles, 60,000 rounds of ammunition, and 500 bombs. Four hundred acres were added to the territories of Anzac. Major-General Cox showed his usual forethought and wisdom.'

The Rangers were relieved at 7.47 a.m. on the 28th August, and left the trenches at 8.30 a.m., and returned to the bivouac behind the Damakjelik Bair.

The roll was called and the numbers in bivouac amounted to 5 officers, viz. :—

Lieut.-Colonel Jourdain (Commanding).

Major Money (Second in Command, and O.C. A and B Companies).

Lieut. R. R. Martin (Acting Adjutant, and O.C. C and D Companies).

2nd Lieut. H. T. Godber (Signalling Officer).

2nd Lieut. C. F. B. Harvey ;

and Lieut. J. I. O'Sullivan, R.A.M.C., who had done splendid service on the previous day, and

Lieut. and Quartermaster P. Farrell, with 208 other ranks.

Major-General Sir A. Godley again visited the Battalion and congratulated them on their gallantry, and said how sorry he was that the Rangers had to give up what they had so gallantly won. He also commended the gallantry of Major Money, and all his men. He hoped the Rangers would soon have another chance of still further distinguishing themselves.

The name of Lieut. S. H. Lewis was submitted to the Brigadier :—

' For gallantry on the 27th August, 1915, when he led the advance party in the attack on the Kaiajik Aghala. This officer was severely wounded on this service, and is now missing.'

(Dispatch 30th August, 1915, O.C. Battalion.)

Major Money did splendid service during the attack on Hill 60, and Lieut. H. T. Godber rendered very good service in charge of the Signallers, whose efforts were most praiseworthy. Lieut. R. R. Martin, who acted as adjutant, discharged his duties in a most efficient way and rendered most useful service.

At 1 a.m. the attack was launched against the Turkish trenches, and these were taken with slight loss, but later the Turks delivered a strong counter-attack and endeavoured to bomb the gallant Light Horse out of their position, but without avail.

The Rangers were in reserve at this attack, but later in the morning of the 29th August at 9 a.m. the enemy began to shell the gully in which the

Rangers then were, but few men were hit, although the fire was very heavy at times. For most of the day and all through the ensuing night the Rangers helped the Australians to improve the hard-won trenches, and to place them in a position to withstand any attack. Two men were wounded that day. At 6 a.m. on the 30th August the Turks began to shell the Well and the approaches to it, and at 9.30 a.m. turned their attention to the hillside, which was the Battalion's bivouac. The hail of shrapnel went on for nearly two hours, and one man was wounded, besides the Commanding Officer of the 5th Ghurkhas (Captain H. T. Molloy), who happened to be passing down the track at that time.

The men of the Battalion worked on at the trenches all through the next night, and also at the sap which it was found necessary to dig near Major-General Cox's Headquarters. The enemy shelled the Battalion's bivouac again on the 31st August, and one man was severely wounded. At 9 p.m. on the evening of the 31st August the Turkish bombers attempted to interfere with the men of the Rangers who were working at the advanced trenches, but were easily repulsed.

Lieut.-Colonel Agnew, who commanded the Brigade, went away to Imbros, and Lieut.-Colonel Jourdain commanded the Brigade from this day until the 2nd September, when Lieut.-Colonel Agnew returned to Headquarters. At 6.45 a.m. on the 1st September the enemy's guns shelled the Battalion's position, and after a pause of an hour or so commenced again at 10 a.m.

The few remaining duty men were working nearly all through the previous night at the sap near the quarters of the G.O.C. No. 6, Section of defence. Some rain fell the previous night, but nearly all men had their great-coats now. 2nd Lieut. H. T. Godber left the Battalion the same day with sickness, and was afterwards invalided to England. He had done good service with the Signallers since he joined the Battalion. On Thursday, the 2nd September, the enemy began to shell the Rangers' position at 7.15 a.m. The first shell fell short and did no harm, but a few seconds later a second shell exploded over the Battalion Headquarters, and wounded Major Money and 8 N.C.O.s and men of the Rangers, besides 5 men of other corps, mostly Australians. Major Money was bending down at the time, and a shrapnel bullet entered his head, and he was taken down to the Hospital Ship, about a mile and a quarter away, at once. However, he never regained consciousness, and to the great regret of all ranks of the Connaught Rangers, he died at sea near Malta on the 7th September, universally regretted and esteemed. Major Money had joined the Battalion at Richmond Barracks, Dublin, on the 24th August, 1914, and his work since then had been an unbroken spell of hard and good work for the Regiment to which he had been appointed and which he loved so well. No words can express the value of the work he had done, and the standard of excellence to which he had brought his Company (B). He died unrewarded for his great efforts, but some consolation was afforded to his many friends, when over five months after the sad occurrence, his name was included in the list of those awarded the Distinguished Service Order, and he was mentioned in Dispatches for his gallant share in the Dardanelles operations. The loss of this officer to the Battalion was irreparable.

At 10.50 a.m. on the same date (2nd September) the hostile gunners again shelled the bivouac, but without further loss. The Rangers were warned to hold themselves in readiness to move on the 3rd September to Bauchop's Hill.

A few shells were directed against the Battalion's position at 8 a.m. on the 3rd September, and caused no loss.

Private Hassett, the chaplain's orderly, was, however, wounded near No. 2 Post. The day was exceedingly hot, and not a breath of breeze came up from the sea. 2nd Lieut. Harvey had also left the Battalion and had been admitted to Hospital for sickness. There were at Headquarters now only the following officers :—

Lieut.-Colonel H. F. N. Jourdain (Commanding).
Lieut. R. R. Martin (Acting Adjutant).
Lieut. J. I. O'Sullivan (R.A.M.C.).
Lieut. and Quartermaster P. Farrell.

Of the original officers who had left England with the Battalion :—

6 had been killed in action or died of wounds.

15 had been wounded (3 of whom, 2nd Lieut. Bennett, Lieut. T. S. P. Martin, and 2nd Lieut. T. W. G. Johnson, had been wounded twice).

3 had been sent down as sick to Base or invalided.

2 combatant officers with the Medical Officer and the Quartermaster only remained.

The number of men with the Battalion was now only 134 all ranks available for duty, not including employés at Brigade Headquarters, &c.

The Battalion was ordered to move quietly after dark to their new position at Bauchop's Hill the same evening (3rd September). The Rangers accordingly paraded at 7.30 p.m. and marched in file to Bauchop's Hill, which was reached at 8.20 p.m. The Brigade Headquarters moved at the same time to the bottom of the Gorge in which the Battalion's bivouac was. The kits were brought round by bullock carts drawn by mules, but these did not reach the Rangers' camp until 11 p.m. that night. The next day, 4th September, was spent in preparing new 'dug-outs' for the men, as although many shells fell near the Gully, no men were wounded, and the work of digging in went briskly on. The next day, 5th September, being Sunday, the chaplains celebrated Divine Service early, and work commenced as soon as possible afterwards, and although Turkish snipers during the evening attempted to annoy the men, only one man was wounded this day. The enemy shelled the Wells near the Rangers' bivouac, but there were no casualties. On the 6th September the enemy shelled the Gully, but without effect, and the men were paraded, as digging had been completed, and were drilled, after which inspections were completed. In the meantime, orders had come to send all available men to work at road-making in the Chilak Dere under the 71st Company R.E. The only available men for this duty (50 in number) were dispatched about 9.50 a.m.

This fatigue was ordered to continue both in the morning and in the afternoon, so there was little chance of a rest for either officers or men.

Heavy gun-fire broke out at 4.30 p.m., but none of the shells fell on the Rangers' hill.

A draft of 2 officers of the Scottish Rifles and 102 N.C.O.s and men from the 3rd and 100 from the 4th Battalion arrived on the night of 7th September at 1 a.m.

The draft was paraded and inspected at 8 a.m. on the 7th September by the Commanding Officer, and was then told off to companies. The officers who accompanied this draft were 2nd Lieuts. N. C. Lucas and A. B. Marshall, 3rd Scottish Rifles.

On the previous day one man had been killed on the beach, where he was employed as a store-man, and three men were wounded that day. One of these men was wounded at the Chilak Dere, and two when at the Well.

Aeroplanes were very active on the 7th, and a hostile one fired at some guns near the Rangers' position and many bullets fell into the camp, but no one was hit.

On the 8th September an account of the operations on the 27th August was published in the ' Local News ', in which the good work of the Rangers was much commended. The men of the Battalion were engaged nearly all day road-making in the Chilak Dere.

One man was wounded at the Well by a bullet

on 7th September, but did not report his wound until the next day.   The storeman on the Base kits on the shore was killed by a shell on the 6th September.   He was a man who was well respected in the Battalion, and was exceedingly popular in the Regiment ; his name was Byrne.

Two Taubes came over the lines on the 9th at 10.30 a.m. and 5.30 p.m., but no one was hit. The majority of the Battalion was again put on road-making that day.   Heavy gun-fire went on all day, and the enemy replied by putting some shells into the Battalion's bivouac at 4.30 p.m.

The troops of the 10th Division were again praised in Sir Ian Hamilton's special order of the 7th September.

Intimation was conveyed to Lieut.-Colonel Jourdain by Lieut.-Colonel Agnew, then in command of the 29th Brigade, that he had been appointed to command the 29th Brigade, and orders arrived for Colonel Agnew to proceed to Mudros.   This took place on the 9th September.

On the following day Captain G. J. B. E. Massy arrived back from the Base, and from hospital after being wounded on 10th August, and took over command of the Battalion.   Lieut.-Colonel Jourdain took over command of the 29th Brigade on the 10th September.   The command of the Brigade was at first permanent, but two days afterwards this was altered, and Lieut.-Colonel Jourdain was placed in temporary command only. The enemy bombarded the lines very heavily at 11 a.m. on the 10th, evidently in retaliation for the shelling to which they had been subjected some hours before.   The men of the Battalion were still employed on the extremely dangerous work in the Chilak Dere. Two men were severely wounded on the 10th, one seriously.

2nd Lieut. Lucas left the Battalion and joined the Royal Irish Rifles.

On the 11th September three more men were wounded, one very seriously in the chest.   Drill, bombing practice, and musketry drills were inaugurated on the 2nd September, and were kept up daily for all men not on actual fatigue.   Early in the day on 12th September two men were wounded, one of whom died almost at once of his wounds. Some rain fell the same evening, but did not last very long.   On the 13th September one wounded man died in Hospital near No. 2 Post of wounds.   Work went on as usual in the Chilak Dere.

The Turks shelled the proximity of the camp heavily at 9 a.m., but no shells fell among the ' dug-outs '.

As the work in the Chilak Dere had now got so dangerous, the work had to be carried on at night for the future (i. e. after the 14th September).

One man was killed on the 14th and 1 wounded.

Heavy rain fell on the night of the 14th September, but the weather cleared up again on the 15th September.   Many shells fell near the Rangers' bivouac, but luckily no shells took effect; one man was wounded by rifle fire on the 15th September.

Captain B. R. Cooper rejoined the Battalion from sick leave on the 16th September, and

took over command from Captain Massy. Lieut.-
General Sir B. T. Mahon came over from Lala
Baba to-day to Bauchop's Hill, and the Brigade-
Major was informed that a Brigadier was being
sent out from England to command the 29th
Brigade.

At 5.5 p.m. on the 18th September exceedingly
heavy fire broke out, and the camp of the Battalion was subjected to the enemy's rifle fire
until 5.25 p.m.   All troops were ordered to stand
to and to be prepared to move at short notice.
At 6.30 p.m. this order was countermanded, and
firing practically ceased at 5.25 p.m.   The Turks
demonstrated against the 9th Corps and 10th
Division also on this day.

2nd Lieut. T. W. G. Johnson was awarded
the Military Cross in the Force orders of the
18th September (List No. 27).

The men who had come out in the new drafts
from England had shown a keenness to rival
their comrades in the 5th Battalion, but the
scarcity of good N.C.O.s was fast becoming acute.
The last draft was composed of men from all
Battalions of the Rangers, 1st, 2nd, 3rd, and 4th
included.

On the 21st September the precincts of the
Rangers' camp was shelled by the enemy at 8.20
a.m., but no damage was done.   Several deserters
came into the British lines during the past
week.

On the afternoon of the 22nd September Lieut.-
Colonel (Temp. Brig.-General) R. S. Vandeleur,
C.M.G., arrived to take command of the Brigade,

and Lieut.-Colonel Jourdain resumed command of the Battalion the same evening.

The sound of gun-fire seldom ceased for long day after day, and even in the short hours, when the guns abstained from firing, the Turkish sniper was seldom absent, and during the hours of darkness numbers of bullets fell among the resting-place of the Rangers, but there were seldom very many casualties.

Every day large parties were requisitioned for strengthening the defences and making the roads both up the Chilak and Aghyl Dere. On the 24th September 2nd Lieut. W. H. Sargaison joined the Battalion from Corporal 7th Battalion Royal Dublin Fusiliers. The enemy's trenches were shelled by the land batteries at 4.30 p.m. on that date, and at 6 p.m. the bombardment was renewed with redoubled vigour. The Turks, on the other hand, demonstrated with rifle fire at 8 p.m., which did not cease until 8.30 p.m. Two orderlies at Brigade Headquarters were wounded, and many bullets fell into the bivouac.

The following officers joined the Battalion to-day at 12.20 a.m. with the draft of 350 other ranks :—

Lieut. R. G. White, 7th Royal Dublin Fusiliers.

2nd Lieut. C. E. Gallwey, 6th Royal Dublin Fusiliers.

2nd Lieut. H. C. Bell, 7th Royal Dublin Fusiliers.

2nd Lieut. G. F. Macnie, 6th Royal Dublin Fusiliers.

2nd Lieut. J. O. N. McKenna, 6th Royal
Dublin Fusiliers.

2nd Lieut. D. M. Fraser was posted to the
Battalion from the ranks of the 7th Royal Dublin
Fusiliers, but did not join the Battalion.

On the 25th September Lieut. R. R. Martin
was admitted to hospital, and Captain Massy took
over the duties of Adjutant from this date.
Lieut. Martin had served with the Battalion since
its arrival on the Peninsula, and had done good
work.

Lieut. - Colonel Jourdain, Lieut. O'Sullivan,
R.A.M.C., and Lieut. and Quartermaster P. Farrell
were the only officers who had served continuously
with the Battalion since the Rangers landed in
Mudros in July 1915.

After celebration of Divine Service on the
26th September, the Brigadier inspected the new
draft and complimented the Battalion on the
turn-out of the men.

One man was wounded on duty on the 26th in
the Chilak Dere.

On the 27th September the Rangers were
ordered to be in readiness to move to Suvla on
the 29th September, instead of to Imbros, which
had at first been arranged. At 7.30 p.m. on the
same date a heavy fire broke out in the trench
line, and bullets began to rain over the lines of
the Rangers, and two men were wounded. This
eventually ceased at 8.15 p.m.

Orders arrived on the 28th September for the
Battalion to march to Suvla on the 29th, and
on arrival there to be prepared to embark in

H

about two days for Imbros to reorganize and rest. These orders were soon afterwards countermanded, and instructions that the Brigade should proceed to Mudros were issued.

Before 7 a.m. on the 29th September, special orders came for the Rangers to march to Anzac the same evening and to embark there for Mudros. All kits and baggage were ordered to be taken with units. The usual bombardment began about 5 p.m., but ceased after about twenty minutes this evening. A large shell, however, fell in front of the guard, but luckily did not explode. At 8.45 p.m. the men of the 5th Battalion fell in and began to move slowly down to the beach at Anzac. The Rangers were due at Walker's Pier at 10 p.m., when 600 men were to embark. The remainder were to proceed with the 10th Hampshire Regiment at 12 o'clock. All kits had been sent down, before the Battalion paraded to move away, to the dump on the shore at Anzac. In the darkness the men of the Rangers began to move down towards No. 2 Post and the sap to Anzac, through which they had first come on the 10th August. Few, however, of those who first trod the dust on that hot August morning returned to Mudros with the Battalion.

Of combatant officers the Commanding Officer had served continuously with the Battalion, and Captain Massy had been only one month absent from wounds, and Captain Cooper had been sick for just over a month, while the Medical Officer, Lieut. O'Sullivan, had never been absent from duty, and the Quartermaster had served throughout all the trying times on the Peninsula. The Rev. T. J. O'Connor, Chaplain to the Brigade, accompanied the Battalion, determined never to be separated from the men he knew and loved so well.

Before night fell a Taube fired at some guns near where the Battalion was located, but no casualties were sustained by the Rangers. This night the sea was calm and there was a warm cool breeze only, while a bright moon later helped the troops in their embarkation. Walker's Pier was reached at 9.45 p.m., but it became necessary to wait for the baggage to be loaded first, and although all this was piled into one single lighter, and thus all the kits of the four regiments of the Brigade became mixed up, the Battalion could not even begin embarkation until 1.20 a.m.

The majority of the Rangers with Headquarters reached the troop-carrier   at 2.20 a.m. There was only room enough to lie down, but soon all ranks were fast asleep. The continual crack of the rifles on Walker's Ridge and Russell's Top went on ceaselessly, but no man was hit, and the steamer left Anzac Cove in the early hours of the morning of the 30th September, and reached Mudros without incident at 8 a.m., just as the sun broke fresh over the surrounding hills and the band of the nearest battleship played the National Anthem, followed by the Marseillaise.

The work of disembarkation began almost at once, and the first boatloads reached the Egyptian Pier at 9.25 a.m., and were ordered to march almost at once to their camp, which was reached at 10.20 a.m.   Here tents, in a certain proportion to each Battalion, were issued and were soon pitched by the men.   The camp was situated on the east side of the harbour, and on the opposite side to that on which the Battalion had been located in July.

Lieut.-General Altham, C.B., C.M.G., and Major-General C. R. McGrigor, C.B., came to visit the Battalion and congratulated the Commanding Officer on the fine performance of the Battalion during its service on the Peninsula.

Much delay was caused by the very unnecessary allocation and alteration of camping-grounds, which kept the men most of the day changing from one piece of ground to another.   That night officers and men, most of whom were accommodated in tents, slept as they had never done for nearly two months.

Orders were received for the men to be re-clothed in service dress, and for the drill khaki and helmets to be returned to store.

The next day (1st October) was spent in indenting for supplies to complete the Battalion with clothing and equipment, as little could be drawn from the Australian and New Zealand Division, and many of the men were wearing the same clothing they had taken into wear in July.

The losses sustained by the Battalion on the Peninsula were as follows :—

Losses up to and including 20th August:—

[1] Officers wounded	6
Officers sick	1
Other ranks killed	15
Other ranks wounded	120
Other ranks sick	78

Losses on 21st and 22nd August:—

Officers killed	3
Officers wounded	9
Warrant Officer wounded . . .	1
Other ranks killed	43
Other ranks wounded	158
[2] Other ranks missing	47
Other ranks sick	7

Losses between 22nd and 27th August:—

Other ranks wounded	3

Losses on the 27th and 28th August:—

1 officer wounded and 1 officer wounded and missing	2
Other ranks killed and wounded . .	152

Losses since 28th August and up to 30th September:—

Officers wounded and since died of wounds	1
Officers sick and in hospital . . .	2
Other ranks killed	4
Other ranks wounded	32
Total all ranks . .	684

[1] One since died of wounds.
[2] Six only reported prisoners in Turkey.

1915   The above total 684 does not include the numbers sent to hospital for sickness after 21st August, or those sent away for various other duties, which amounted to nearly 127. Thirty officers, including the Chaplain, embarked for the Peninsula, and four only remained at the end of August, not including the Chaplain.

29 *Officers and* 1 *Chaplain, with* 945 *other ranks, embarked on* 9th *July for the Peninsula.*

1 man died at sea.

684 were killed, wounded, missing or sick, including officers. Remaining with Battalion, 162.

Other losses by sickness, detachment or to Base, or accidentally injured, &c., not accounted for above.

ORDERS FOR TROOPS ARRIVING IN ANZAC

AUGUST, 1915

Organization Orders for the Troops in Anzac.

The following orders are published, so that troops may make provision now for the various steps required.

Dress and Equipment.   1.—The dress for operations will be :—

F.S. equipment, less great-coats and packs. Respirators will be carried.

Ammunition, 200 rounds per man carried on person.

Machine guns—3,500 rounds per gun in belt boxes.

No regimental or brigade reserve will accompany

the troops, but will be sent forward later as required from the reserves which have been formed.

Trained bomb-throwers will be included in each company.

Those men will carry only 50 rounds of ammunition, but will each be provided with an additional haversack to carry 8 bombs.

Sandbags. At least one per man.

Tools. The light entrenching tool will be carried, and in addition picks and shovels in the proportion of one pick and one shovel to each eight men—carried on person. (One pick and one shovel per four men not employed in an attacking column.)

Wire-cutters will be carried. Other articles of equipment at the discretion of Commanders in charge of special operations.

All Red and Yellow Semaphore Flags.—Signalling or special issue in possession of units are to be taken. One each per officer and N.C.O. up to the number in possession, after deducting signalling requirements. Those red and yellow flags are to be waved rapidly when it is desired to show the position of our troops to the Navy, our own artillery, or to the infantry.

Water Bottles.—Filled and to be very sparingly used.

Iron Rations.—Meat and biscuits or equivalent; one day.

· Groceries, two days.

Indian ranks. Goor or sugar in place of groceries.

All ranks will wear *white armlets*, 6 inches wide,

1915 fixed on each arm above the elbow, and a *white patch* about 8 inches square fixed on the back of the right shoulder or between the shoulder-blades. This will be worn in addition to any distinguishing marks selected by Commanders of columns.

No animals will be available for carriage of any equipment. Cable and other technical equipment usually carried in carts or wagons is to be carried on barrows or by hand.

Night Opera-tions. 2. The pass word for night operations will be published in operation orders.

Any one not answering with the countersign at once, and any one without the distinguishing armlets and patch ordered in paragraph 1, will be treated as an enemy.

The following refers to night operations involving a night march previous to assault :—

i. Rifles are not to be loaded. Magazines will not be charged before moving off, and are only to be charged by the direct order of an officer.

ii. Bayonets will be fixed.

iii. All movement is to be as silent as possible : guides and leaders of columns are reminded that a pace of more than a mile an hour cannot be attained in broken country with a column of more than 500 men.

iv. No talking is to be permitted from the hour of falling in till daylight : necessary orders are to be passed in low tones.

v. No smoking or lights are to be permitted from the hour of falling in till daylight.

vi. No messenger is to be sent from front to

rear at a faster pace than the column is moving, as men moving rapidly back are apt to cause panic. Unless, therefore, the matter is urgent the messenger should be dropped to await the arrival of the person the message is meant for. Similarly, no evacuation of wounded to the rear during darkness is to take place till the columns have passed by. No man not a stretcher-bearer is to fall out on the excuse of assisting wounded to the rear unless his services have been demanded by the medical officer.

vii. In the event of the enemy's fire being opened while troops are moving on the objective, troops are to move on, advanced parties or special groups being detailed for attacking enemy picquets or snipers with the bayonet if those are close to the line of march.

If the fire is effective, as from machine-gun fire trained on a point, troops will take cover while steps are organized to deal with it.

When, however, the objective is close, troops will press on to its capture at all costs, remembering that several other columns are aiming at the same objective, and that the attack of one aids all.

viii. Electric torches, used only by officers and by the order of the senior Commander on the spot, will be useful to flash backwards and show position of front lines from time to time to those in rear. (These are only for use once touch with the enemy has been gained and the advance of the troops can no longer be concealed.)

ix. When considering the distribution of troops in their commands, leaders are warned that soon

1915 rather than late, enemy picquets will be met with. Each column should therefore be headed by a party ready to deal without any hesitation with an enemy party when met with—using the bayonet and following up quickly on the heels of the enemy if he withdraws up the direction of the march.

Dis-posal of Surplus Equip-ment. 3. In accordance with paragraph 1, packs and other articles of equipment have to be left behind. This applies to all units, as whether employed actively or passively to begin with, all may be required to assume the offensive at short notice.

Those articles will be collected before falling in and left in charge of a party of

1 officer per brigade.

1 senior N.C.O. per Battalion.

2 men per Company.

And a similar proportion for other units.

This equipment, with all surplus kit, will be left: in the case of new arrivals—in the area allotted to the units, under Brigade arrangements; in the case of Anzac units—as may be selected under Divisional arrangements.

Dis-posal of Sick. 4. Casualties occurring in the Brigade area between dark of the night on which movement commences and the march of troops will be dealt with under arrangements which are being made for all troops by Australian Division in their area, and New Zealand and Australian Division in theirs. None but urgent cases will be evacuated until daylight.

Water. 5. The afternoon before operations commence an extra supply of water will be provided for troops detailed for operations beyond the Anzac

position.   Water-bottles are to be filled from this.
As much as possible of any balance from this extra
issue should be consumed before starting.

6. All ranks are to be warned to be sparing in *Care of*
their use of water, food, and ammunition.   In *Sup-*
some cases there is no possibility of water being *plies.*
sent up to the troops for at least eighteen hours
after their movement commences, nor of food
being available for forty-eight hours.   Any food
or water thrown away cannot therefore be re-
placed.

As regards ammunition, every effort will be
made to bring up reserves immediately in the rear
of troops, but none the less wild firing is to be
checked at once and no firing permitted except
on paying targets—or by picked shots specially
detailed to deal with individual enemy.

7. All ranks are also to be warned that the first *Rest.*
night of the operations will be sleepless and the
next probably sleepless also.   They should therefore during the night and day preceding the operations rest rather than move about unnecessarily.

8. All new arrivals are reminded that no labour *En-*
expended on digging is started and that when they *trench-*
occupy a position they are to work, not till they *ing.*
have completed a little breastwork, but till a deep
recessed fire trench has been made.   Then they are
to continue till supports and communication
trenches are complete and give full protection
against shrapnel and small arm fire.   And as the
only tools available will be those carried by the
men, these are on no account to be thrown away
because of their weight or inconvenience.

9. The troops employed are armed with rifles firing two marks of ammunition, mark VI and mark VII.

The maxim built for the mark VI cannot take mark VII ammunition—and this is being legislated for as far as possible by employing guns now at Anzac in places where only mark VI ammunition is used by the troops.

Mark VII ammunition can be used in any mark of ·303 rifle, but is likely to jam in loading and a different sighting is necessary. Briefly—L. E. short rifle or the long rifle using mark VII ammunition fires high up to 400 yards and after that low. A rifle sighted for mark VII ammunition and using mark VI ammunition fires low for the first 400 yards and after that high.

It is therefore desirable to avoid mixing up the two marks, and to help in this, boxes of mark VII ammunition are clearly marked, and have in addition two ' V '-shaped nicks on the ends of the lids of all boxes, so that the boxes can be distinguished by feel as well as by sight. An additional safeguard is that all mark VII ammunition is packed in bandoleers for convenience in distribution, and not in packets.

III

RECORD OF THE 5TH (SERVICE) BATTALION THE CONNAUGHT RANGERS

FROM 2ND OCTOBER, 1915, TO 10TH JANUARY, 1916.

THE Battalion remained at Mudros East from the 30th September to the 5th October. On the 2nd October the Battalion was warned to be ready for a sudden move that day or on the day following. The day was exceedingly hot and sultry, and dysentery had increased in an alarming manner among the men since the arrival of the Battalion in the Island of Lemnos.

The following order was published this evening :—

' The Brigadier-General Commanding has much pleasure in publishing the attached letter from Major-General Sir A. Godley, K.C.M.G., C.B., referring to the good work of the Brigade at Anzac.

Brigade order dated 2–10–15, by Brig.-General R. S. Vandeleur, C.M.G.'

> New Zealand and Australian Division,
> Divisional Headquarters,
> No. 2 Post,
> 29th September, 1915.

MY DEAR VANDELEUR,

On the departure of your Brigade from Anzac, I must write a line to let you know how much I and every one in this Division appreciated the work which has been done by your Brigade while it has been attached to us since 7th August.

The taking of the Kabak Kuyu Wells by the Connaught Rangers, and their share in the attack on the Kaiajik Aghala, worthily upheld the traditions of that distinguished Regiment, and the work of the Leinster Regiment at Quinn's Post and Russell's Top has been excellent throughout. The Royal Irish Rifles and Hampshire Regiment plunged at short notice into the thick of a considerable battle, suffered casualties such as well might have destroyed the morale and efficiency of those Battalions, but the excellent work which they have since done and the efforts which they have made to restore their efficiency makes certain that they will give a good account of themselves when they next meet the Turk.   I should be very glad if you will convey to all ranks of your Brigade my thanks for the work they have done for this Division.

Yours sincerely,

(Sd.) A. GODLEY,

Major-General.

Commanding New Zealand and Australian Division.

Brig.-General Vandeleur, C.M.G.

Commanding 29th Infantry Brigade.

At 6 p.m. on the 2nd October two drafts reached the camp of the Battalion, one of thirty-four N.C.O.s and men who had returned from hospital, both sick and wounded, and 148 of the draft who had been detained at Mudros, and who had arrived from England by the same troopship as the 350 men who had joined on the 24th September.   All the troops attended service at 6.45 a.m. on the 3rd October, and afterwards the preparations for completing the clothing of the Battalion were pressed on.

Many of the men and some officers had been allowed to grow beards on the Peninsula, but the Brigadier now ordered all beards to be removed at once.   On the 4th October the Brigade was ordered to parade for a route march at 8.35 a.m.   After a tiring march of some five miles, during which the Brigade was halted and formed up many times, the force reached a point about two miles from camp, when suddenly orders were received to embark at 2 p.m.   This was at about 11.15 a.m., and the Rangers were then quite two miles from camp, on a rough tract of open country.   The Battalion was at once marched home, and reached camp at about 11.50 a.m.   Here information was received that the Battalion would not embark that day, but the Irish Rifles and Leinsters would embark at 2 p.m.

The other two Regiments left in the afternoon, and Lieut.-Colonel Jourdain was left behind in command of the two Battalions (the Rangers and the 10th Hampshire Regiment) which would embark on the 5th October.   2nd Lieut. McKenna rejoined the 6th Royal Dublin Fusiliers on 4th October, and 2nd Lieut. J. M. Sinclair joined the Battalion from the 13th (Service) Battalion Scottish Rifles.

The morning of the 5th October was exceedingly

hot and sultry, and the men suffered very much from the oppressive heat in the new serge clothing.

Helmets and khaki drill clothing had been left behind, and were for the most part burnt by the Ordnance afterwards. The Rangers paraded at 9.35 a.m. to march down to the Egyptian Pier for embarkation to an unknown destination. The Battalion was embarked partly on the   , and partly on the   , the party on the latter vessel being mostly A Company under Captain B. R. Cooper. The Headquarters and the other companies proceeded in the   , on which they embarked at 12.30 p.m. Nine officers, including Lieut.-Colonel Jourdain, the Medical Officer, and the Chaplain and 497 other ranks, embarked in the   . Captain Cooper, with the greater part of his own and C Company, embarked just before on the   . The Divisional Staff and the Staff of the 30th Brigade proceeded in the troopship   . At 9.30 p.m. this ship commenced to move out of the harbour, but almost directly ran into the outer boom and at once let down anchor and remained stationary for the night. The work of cutting the ship out began the morning of the 6th October, and it was not completed until 1.20 p.m. on the same date. Then the transport moved back into the inner harbour, and anchored again at 2 p.m.

Lieut.-General Sir B. Mahon and Staff departed on H.M. Destroyer *Lawford* at 3.20 p.m., and having been called back by wireless, returned to the ship at 7.35 p.m.

The   was one of the Ocean Steamship
Company's vessels, and was of 10,049 tons dis-
placement.   Later in the day the   steamed
up the harbour and anchored again at 6 p.m.,
all troops remaining on board ship that night.

On the 7th October the Headquarters of the
30th Brigade, and the 6th Royal Munster Fusiliers
and 7th Royal Dublin Fusiliers were taken off the
ship and encamped on shore ; and Lieut.-Colonel
Jourdain, as O.C. troops, with the 5th Connaught
Rangers and 6th Royal Dublin Fusiliers and some
details, remained on board the   .

Lieut.-General Sir Bryan Mahon left the ship
with his staff and proceeded to Salonika in H.M.S.
Louis.

At 7.45 p.m. the   , having dragged her
anchor owing to the storm which was raging at the
time, drifted on to a mine-sweeper, and the railing
round the saloon deck and the saloon window of
the vessel were smashed.   However, before much
damage was done, the two ships were drawn apart,
and later the P. and O. transport   was
moored alongside.   The troops on shore were
drenched through, and spent a very wretched night
without cover of any kind.   On the 9th October
the remainder of the troops were brought back to
the ship soon after 9 a.m., and at 5.20 p.m. the
transport began to move down the harbour, and
at 6.30 p.m. was outside the bar.

Lieut.-Colonel Jourdain was requested by Brig.-
General Nicol to retain command of the troops on
board ship.

All lights were extinguished after dark, and the

steamed for Salonika, escorted by a cruiser and a destroyer.

At 6.15 a.m. on the 10th October, the transport began to enter the Gulf of Salonika, and reached the boom at 8 a.m. The town of Salonika showed forth plainly in the morning sun, a very beautiful sight from the sea.

After some hours' delay, the Rangers were ordered at 12.15 p.m. to disembark at 1.30 p.m. with the Divisional Signal Company. With the aid of the naval transport authorities this was soon accomplished, and the first party of 350 men reached the Docks at 2.5 p.m.

All baggage was on shore by 4.10 p.m., and transport was also requisitioned and was ready by that hour. The Battalion then began the march to the camp about 2½ miles outside the town, and near a farm called Lembet. The Brigade camp was pitched on a ridge, and the remainder of the Battalion was in camp here under Captain B. R. Cooper. The view of the Gulf and the town was exceedingly fine, and Mount Olympus, then covered with snow, formed a most picturesque and beautiful background.

The disembarkation of the French Army was also proceeding rapidly at the time, and the main road to the camp was crowded with Greek and French troops.

The mobilization of the Greek Army was then proceeding rapidly, and the long lines of baggage animals were continually moving both to and away from Salonika to the camps near Lake Langaza and Kirechkeui.

The Rangers reached their camp at 6.5 p.m., after a hot and very tiring march, and both officers and men loaded down with heavy marching order, and all blankets and waterproof sheets in addition, as no transport could be provided for these articles: an arrangement that was both unnecessary and absurd.

About 300 men were left on fatigue duty at the docks, and these did not arrive in camp until 4.20 p.m. on the next day (the 11th October).

The 30th Brigade began to arrive at Lembet Camp at 8.20 a.m. on the 11th October. The Battalion was afterwards exercised daily, and the equipment of the troops was pushed on as fast as stores could be obtained. These were, however, very meagre, and little could be obtained from Salonika. Eight horses were issued to the Battalion on the 13th October, but six of these were withdrawn some days later.

The French troops meanwhile arrived in large numbers, and were pushed on up country from the military station situated along the Monastir Road.

On the 15th October heavy rain began to fall, and continued for several days ; the camp became a sea of mud, and although the troops were under canvas, the conditions of camp life were anything but comfortable.

The same day a draft under 2nd Lieut. D. P. J. Kelly with 2nd Lieuts. G. Robinson and H. J. Shanley arrived in the evening, with 276 other ranks, which brought the strength of the 5th Battalion up to 1,078 other ranks, excluding officers.

1915   There were present at Headquarters the following officers :—

Lieut.-Colonel H. F. N. Jourdain (Commanding).

Captain B. R. Cooper.

Captain G. J. B. E. Massy (Adjutant).

2nd Lieut. D. P. J. Kelly.

2nd Lieut. C. F. B. Harvey (who had rejoined at Mudros from hospital).

2nd Lieut. G. Robinson.

2nd Lieut. H. J. Shanley.

2nd Lieut. W. H. Sargaison.

Lieut. J. I. O'Sullivan, R.A.M.C. (Medical Officer).

Lieut. and Quartermaster P. Farrell ;

and the following attached officers :—

Lieut. R. G. White, 7th R.D.F.

2nd Lieut. C. E. Gallwey, 6th R.D.F.

2nd Lieut. H. C. Bell, 7th R.D.F.

2nd Lieut. G. F. Macnie, 6th R.D.F.

2nd Lieut. A. B. Marshall, 3rd Scot. Rifles.

2nd Lieut. T. Skene, 13th Scot. Rifles.

2nd Lieut. J. M. Sinclair, 13th Scot. Rifles.

2nd Lieuts. D. J. Cowan and H. H. L. Richards of the 5th Connaught Rangers joined the Battalion on the 16th October. Lieut. V. J. Tibbs joined the Battalion a few days later.

Rain continued to pour down ceaselessly throughout the 16th, 17th, and 18th October, and the whole country was a sea of mud and water. The Brigade was ordered to parade several times for a route march, and the men generally came back to camp wet through with no possibility of a change.

On the 20th October the Battalion paraded at 9.30 a.m. and marched in Brigade to the pass between the hills near Langaza Lake. The transport with the men's dinners had started at 7.30 a.m. As the Brigade marched off, the rain came down in torrents, and continued to do so until the end of the march was reached at 12 o'clock.

As soon as the men's dinners were ready, they were served up, and all Battalions were ordered to march home independently.

The Rangers began to march home at 1.35 p.m., reaching camp at 3.47 p.m., and although on the return journey the weather kept up for a time, at 5.30 p.m. the same evening rain came down again and the whole camp was in an appalling state.

The distance marched on the 20th was twelve miles.

On the 21st October a few more tents were obtained for the Battalion, and many who were very much crowded before were able to sleep now about fifteen in a tent.

Captain Cooper was admitted to hospital this day, and was later sent by ship to Egypt. A gale with much rain raged throughout the night of the 21st October and the early morning of the 22nd, and the weather was very cold, many of the tents being blown down by the force of the gale.

The state of the camp was simply appalling, and the mud was even more than two feet deep between the lines. Everything was wet and all the soldiers' clothing was drenched through and through. More rain fell on the evening of the 22nd October.

A Brigade route march to Kirechkeui and back

1915 commenced at 9 a.m. on the 23rd October, and after a short halt under the towering height of Beaz Tash (2,193 feet high), the return march was begun, and the Brigade reached camp in fine weather at 2.20 p.m., having marched twelve miles.

The Rangers were now ordered to hand over all transport to the 30th Brigade to complete them at once before they began to entrain for Serbia.

Rain, which had held off for the last twenty-two hours, commenced to fall again soon after 8 p.m. the same evening, and the state of the camp was very bad, and all clothing was saturated by the rain.

On the 24th October a farewell order was promulgated to the troops, which is here given in detail :—

FAREWELL ORDER BY
GENERAL SIR IAN HAMILTON.

General Headquarters,
Mediterranean Expeditionary Force,
October 17th, 1915.

' On handing over the Command of the Mediterranean Expeditionary Force to General Sir C. C. Monro, the Commander-in-Chief wishes to say a few farewell words to the Allied troops, with many of whom he has now for so long been associated. First, he would like them to know his deep sense of the honour it has been to command so fine an Army in one of the most arduous and difficult Campaigns which has ever been undertaken ; secondly, he must express to them

his admiration at the noble response which they 1915
have invariably given to the calls he has made
upon them. No risk has been too desperate ;
no sacrifice too great. Sir Ian Hamilton thanks
all ranks, from Generals to private soldiers, for
the wonderful way they have seconded his efforts
to lead them towards that decisive victory, which,
under their new Chief, he has the most implicit
confidence they will achieve.'

The Battalion was sent out on a route march
of about six miles on the 25th October, but rain
compelled a return to camp at 12.35 p.m.

The day broke on the 26th October with
torrential rain still falling, and hour after hour
passed with the same phenomenal fall of rain,
and it was not until 11.40 a.m. that the weather
cleared up somewhat.

All horses except two had been given up this
day to the 30th Brigade. 2nd Lieut. A. C. Holmes
joined the Battalion on the 26th with 32 men of
the Rangers' transport from England ; these men
had been left behind when the Battalion left
Basingstoke in July. The Brigade, including the
Rangers, were marched in Brigade to the Derbend
Pass, and returned to camp the same afternoon.
On the return march the 15th Mountain Battery
and the 9th Field Battery of the Greek Army
were passed on the march towards the frontier.
The length of the march was twelve miles.

The Battalion was inspected by the Officer
Commanding the Brigade in marching order at
12.5 p.m. on the 29th October, and the Brigadier

informed the Commanding Officer that the Battalion was better turned out than the other battalions of the Brigade which he had inspected, and also that the packs were well packed, and that he was much pleased with the general turn-out of the Battalion.

The 6th and 7th Royal Dublin Fusiliers had left for the front, their destination being unknown.

One man of the Rangers died in hospital on the 29th October.

On the 30th October the Battalion marched in Brigade with all first line of transport on the road to Kirechkeui for a distance of nearly four miles, and returned to camp by the same route.

The other two regiments of the 30th Brigade moved down to the military station that day, and went away early on the 31st October.

On the 3rd November the Rangers took part in a Brigade field-day in the neighbourhood of Eurenjik, and returned to camp at 4.30 p.m. The fifes which had been purchased in Salonika and the drums which had been recovered from the Ordnance were taken out on this field-day, and elicited the admiration of the other regiments. The march was only seven miles on this occasion. Very heavy rain fell on the 4th November.

Field operations by the Brigade took place on the 5th November, when the day's work did not conclude until 5.20 p.m., and the Battalion reached camp after a seven-mile march and trench-digging in the hills near Lembet.

On the 8th November the Brigade was ordered to march in full marching order to the Derbend

defile.   There was a celebration and review in
Salonika on this day in honour of St. Demetrius,
the patron saint of Salonika, and many Greek
officers and others were coming into Salonika for
the occasion, and passed the Brigade *en route.*
Lieut.-Colonel Jourdain commanded the Brigade
in place of the Brigadier, who was sick.   Captain
Massy commanded the Battalion.

Field operations with a night march on the
evening of the 9th November, and the early
morning of the 10th, kept the Battalion on the
hills near Lembet until 9.20 a.m. on the latter
date.   2nd Lieut. F. W. Illingworth, 12th Scottish
Rifles, and 2nd Lieut. J. A. Calderwood, 4th
Scottish Rifles, and 71 other ranks (all Connaught
Rangers), joined the Battalion this day soon after
their arrival back in camp.

The last Regiment of the 31st Brigade went
away on the same day to the Serbian border.

Orders were received on the 11th November
that the Battalion would probably move up to
the Serbian border on the 15th November.

Mules and limber wagons to make up to scale
were ordered to be drawn at once.

On the 12th November the 6th Leinster Regiment and one Company of the Irish Rifles marched
to the military station to entrain the next day.
The Brigadier and Staff left on the 13th November,
and Lieut.-Colonel Jourdain was left in command
of the remainder of the Brigade at Salonika.

On the 14th November orders were received
for the Battalion to march to the military station
the same afternoon, and to entrain at 6 a.m.

on the 15th November. Kits were at once packed, and the Battalion paraded at 3.15 p.m. and marched close to the French lines to the military station on the Monastir road, which was reached at 5.10 p.m. As the Battalion marched past the French lines, the drums struck up ' Killaloe ' and the ' Marseillaise ', which delighted the French troops, who not only cheered and joined in the chorus, but embraced the big drummer in their delight. The two green flags with a huge harp, which were carried by two companies, were received with great ceremony, and not only were saluted by many of the French soldiers, but were saluted by the guards also, who turned out and presented arms in a most deferential manner, thinking they were the colours of the Battalion.

The Battalion went into bivouac until 3.30 a.m. on the 15th November, when breakfast was partaken of by the dim light of a candle, in the Headquarters Mess, as the early morning was both cold and dark. The transport of the Battalion was timed to entrain at 4 a.m., and the Battalion at 6 a.m.

However, at 6 a.m. it was still quite dark and no troop train was available anywhere. It was not until 6.34 a.m. that the first streaks of daylight made it possible for the transport to make its way down to the military siding, and even then no trucks or carriages were available until nearly 7 a.m. The Battalion marched down with drums playing at 7.30 a.m., and reaching the station at 7.35 a.m., entrained at once, all ranks being on the train soon after 7.45 a.m.

The train remained until 8.10 a.m., when it began to move northwards. The men were accommodated in vans, and all the officers were put into a second-class carriage. The second portion of the transport was detailed to come by a second train leaving at 2 p.m. the same day, together with 40 N.C.O.s and men, all of the transport. The strength of the Rangers proceeding up to Serbia should have been 996 other ranks, but owing to several men reporting sick and other causes, the actual strength was a little over 970.

One officer, 2nd Lieut. Calderwood, was left behind at the Base detail camp with the surplus men, and 2nd Lieut. Skene also reported sick and was left behind. Both these officers belonged to the Scottish Rifles.

At 8.25 a.m. the troop-train crossed the Vardar river, by the side of which many small gardens lay; this river ran for many miles almost parallel to the railway line. The side of the river was also bordered by several hundred yards of sedge and marsh.

A station called Karaoglu was reached and passed at 9.20 a.m., and at 10.10 a.m. Karasauli station. Here the train waited for nearly an hour, but as the day was now quite warm, the time passed very quickly, and some chickens were purchased by the men from the few Greek inhabitants who occupied the houses near the station. Here were Greek guards spending a very lazy and idle existence.

The view from the train towards the mountains on the western side was very beautiful, and the hills looked quite blue in the morning sun. In many of the stations passed the houses were still very much knocked about and shot-riddled, having never been repaired since the last Balkan War. The Greek inhabitants continually tried to sell ' koniak ' to the soldiers, and this entailed constant vigilance to prevent the spirit being passed into the carriages.

Karasauli was left behind at 11.10 a.m., and after going a short distance to the south the railway commenced to go northwards by the western shore of Ardzan Lake. The western shore of the Amatovo Lake had been passed before arrival at Karasauli.

The maps of this part of Macedonia which had been issued to the troops were all of German origin, and all names were inserted in German on them. At 11.50 a.m. the blue range of the Bellashitza Mountains showed through a gap in the hills, and the cloud effect on this high range was very grand.

Trenches, white crosses, and other signs of the conflict in the last Balkan War were very apparent along the route to Dojran, especially before the train reached Kilindir station at 12.10 p.m. The train proceeded slowly over a bridge that had been damaged during the recent floods, and steamed into Kilindir station.

Here a Bulgarian, who could not speak a word of English, was brought to the Commanding Officer by an English-speaking Greek, as he wished to enlist in the Regiment. On being asked why, he said he wished to fight against the

Bulgarians, whom he detested. He was not, however, taken for a Connaught Ranger, and was much
dejected at being rejected.

The journey was resumed at 12.40 p.m., when
the train proceeded on to Dojran, four miles
distant, which was reached at 1.10 p.m. The
view of the Bellashitza Range across the Lake
Dojran was exceedingly picturesque and grand.
The lake was an inland one, containing large
quantities of fish ; and the inhabitants drove a
good trade by netting these fish and selling them
to the soldiers and to the other inhabitants of the
district, needless to say, at an exorbitant price.

The work of unloading the train was excellently
well done, and at 2.10 p.m. every vehicle was
unloaded, and all the mules were safely detrained
and harnessed to the wagons and limbers. The
Railway Transport Officer heartily congratulated
the Battalion on the willingness and smartness of
all ranks during the work of detraining. The
compliment was well deserved. The Battalion
paraded a few minutes afterwards, and marched
to the bivouac about a mile from the station,
which was reached at 3.15 p.m.

The Rangers crossed the Serbian border line
about a quarter of a mile from the bivouac. Here
was a Serbian border guard-house and a Serbian
guard, which looked on with an amused expres-
sion at the troops marching with their drums
and fifes in front. The Brigadier met the Battalion just outside camp, and accompanied it to
the bivouac. The night fell quickly, and almost
as soon as the bivouacs were pitched, the sun

disappeared before 5 p.m. and it was almost dark. There were many shell cases and cartridge cases over the ground where the camp was pitched, the reminiscences of the last Balkan War. The tree trunks were also riddled with shrapnel bullets, which could even be picked out by hand.

Soon after 8 a.m. on the 16th November the sound of gun fire could be heard from the north, where the French were driving back the Bulgarian forces from the ridge near Rabrovo. This was especially heavy at 3 p.m., when the burst of the shells could be plainly seen from the position near Dojran. Firing again broke out at 5 p.m., but the Rangers remained in bivouac this day.

On the 17th November the 6th Leinster Regiment and the 6th Royal Irish Rifles marched away northwards at 9.30 a.m.

The Rangers proceeded out for Battalion exercise at 9.30 a.m., and returned to camp at 12.5 p.m. Some rain fell, and in the evening the weather turned bitterly cold and a gale blew over the lines. In the evening the Rangers were ordered to march at 9.30 a.m. on the morrow. At 6.35 a.m. in the cold and frosty morning the men of the Battalion struck their bivouacs, and after breakfast at 7.30 a.m., paraded at 9.15 a.m., and followed by the 10th Hampshire Regiment marched towards the town of Dojran, which lay about a mile ahead along the road. Headed by the drums of the Rangers, the Battalion marched through the town, which seemed to contain many Turks, but few Serbians. The Serbians saluted and appeared in good spirits, but there was only a sullen look on the remainder of the population, which seemed anything but friendly.

After about an hour's march along the shore of the lake the two Regiments were halted by Lieut.-Colonel Jourdain, who had been delegated to command by the Brigadier, who had gone on ahead. The early morning was cold and frosty, but when the sun came out later the air was quite warm. The two Regiments reached the Brigade Headquarters at 1.30 p.m., having marched a little over 9 miles. The bivouac was soon laid out, and the men, who had carried great-coats, blankets, and waterproof sheets as well as their bivouacs, were soon hard at work cooking their tea. All the bivouacs had also been put up within the short space of a few minutes. Only six men of the Rangers fell out, although many of the other Regiment left the ranks on the march. At first no move was ordered for at least two days, but later (about 8 p.m.) it was announced that a move was in contemplation. It was not until 10.55 p.m. that orders arrived for the two Battalions to march to Rabrovo on the morrow.

The night was exceedingly cold but fine. Reveillé went at 6.30 a.m. on the 19th November, and the Battalion began to march towards the Dedeli Pass at 9 a.m. The bivouac on the 18th was near Hasanli, and was situated in a donga near the main road. The drums were allowed to play until the Dedeli Pass was reached, when it was considered advisable to conceal the movements of the Battalion from the enemy.

2nd Lieut. Harvey was admitted to hospital

and left the Battalion the same day, together with one man. The 10th Hampshires, with Brigade Headquarters, followed at 10 a.m. After traversing the Dedeli Pass, the Rangers reached Rabrovo at 11.5 a.m., and halted in a clearance near the village to let the men cook their dinners.

At 1 p.m. A and B Companies were sent out to take up positions then occupied by the 7th Royal Munster Fusiliers, north-west of the village, and D Company to some second-line trenches almost due north.

Both these positions were quite useless, and could not have been utilized for any purpose whatever. They had been originally made three years ago, but had only been slightly altered since then. The condition of these trenches was very dirty, and one party of B Company had to climb almost to the top of the range above Valandovo. The post occupied by D Company was also very unsatisfactory, but the Battalion was ordered to take up same for that night, and it was accordingly occupied at once. The Brigadier ordered that it should be changed the next day. The Battalion Headquarters with C in reserve were near the village of Rabrovo. The march this day was 4½ miles long.

The Headquarters of the French General (General Bonnot) were at Valandovo.

During the night heavy gun and rifle fire was heard on the left, and the French were reported to have had hard fighting in that direction.

The orders arrived on the evening of the 18th for the 30th and 31st Brigades to take over the

French trenches from the Kozlu Dere to near 1915
Kosturino, and are given here in full :—

10TH DIVISION ORDER NO. I.

18th November, 1915.

I. The 10th Division will relieve the French troops in first line on the night 20–21 November as follows :—

31st Infantry Brigade from the Kozlu Dere through Prstan and Memisli to Rocky Peak just S. of Ormanli.

30th Infantry Brigade from same Rocky Peak exclusive to Kosturino.

Cyclist Company will hold the Knoll on the Serbo-Bulgarian frontier just E. of main Rabrovo-Strumnitza Station.

29th Infantry Brigade will be in General Reserve at Rabrovo less two Battalions respectively at (*a*) Pozarli, (*b*) Causli.

II. The following moves will take place :—

(*a*) The two Battalions 29th Infantry Brigade now on Dojran–Dedeli Road will move to Rabrovo, one Battalion relieving the 7th Royal Munster Fusiliers holding the heights NE., N., and NW. thereof.

The two remaining Battalions 29th Infantry Brigade will relieve the two Battalions of the 31st Infantry Brigade, now holding (*a*) Pozarli, (*b*) Causli–Gokceli Bala.

The Company, 29th Infantry Brigade, now at Dojran will remain there until further orders. These moves to be carried out on the 19th instant.

K

(*b*) 31st Infantry Brigade will be concentrated about Calkali by 1200, 20th instant.

(*c*) The troop Yeomanry will remain at Hasanli covering the right flank.

(*d*) S. A. A. Section 68th F. A. B. Ammunition Column will move to Dedeli on 20th, after 31st Infantry Brigade has cleared the Dojran–Dedeli Road.

III. Brig.-General A. B. Helyar having arrived, he will assume command of the Artillery units of the Division.

IV. The 3 Field Companies and 5th Royal Irish Regiment Pioneers will not move and will continue the work upon which they are now engaged.

V. Reports to Dedeli, after noon, 20th instant. Issued at 1800.

(Sd.)   G. E. LEMAN, Lt.-Col.

General Staff, 10th Division.

The Brigade order is as follows :—

COPY No. 2.

29th Brigade Order No. 3 C., by Brig.-General R. S. Vandeleur, C.M.G., commanding 29th Infantry Brigade.

Ref. Vodena, Sheet 1 : 200.000 map.

18.11.15.

I. The Brigade will carry out the following moves to-morrow :—

> (*a*) The 6th R.I. Rifles to relieve the 6th R.I. Fusiliers in the position above Causli.
>
> (*b*) The 5th Connaught Rangers to relieve

the 7th Royal Munster Fusiliers in 1915
the position above Rabrovo.

(*c*) The 10th Hampshire Regt. to reserve
at Rabrovo.

(*d*) The 6th Leinster Regt. (H.Q. as at
present) to relieve 5th Inniskilling
Fusiliers in position above Pozarli.

(*e*) The Brigade H.Q. and 30th Field
Ambulance to Rabrovo.

II. The 5th Connaught Rangers will march at
0900 to-morrow to Rabrovo, where it will be met
by guides at 1300 and guided to its positions.
The transport will accompany the Battalion.

III. The Brigade H.Q. followed by the 10th
Hampshire Regt. will pass the red flag on the
road at the northern camp boundary at 1000 and
march to Rabrovo. 1st line transport will follow
in rear of the column in the above order.

IV. The 30th Field Ambulance will march in rear
of the Brigade transport leaving camp at 10.30.

V. Orders *re* moves of 6th R.I. Rifles and
6th Leinster Rifles have been issued to them
separately in operation order 3 A and 3 B.

VI. Divisional H.Q. will be at Dedeli from 1200
to-morrow.

(Sd.) T. G. ANDERSON, Major.

B.M., 29th Brigade.

Copy No. 1 to 10th Hampshire Regt. ⎫ by
No. 2 to 5th Connaught Rangers ⎬ orderly.
No. 3 to 30th Field Ambulance ⎭
No. 4 retained.

Out at 21.45.

K 2

1915   On the 20th November, after arrangements had been made to relieve the Company situated above Rabrovo by a Company of the 10th Hampshire Regt. at 8 a.m., orders were received for the Rangers and the 10th Hampshire Regt. to march to Tatarli at once.

A, B, and D Companies were withdrawn from the outpost line, but did not rejoin until nearly 11 a.m., when the Battalion began the march to Tatarli. At 8.30 a.m. the Bulgarian Artillery began to shell the French lines on Hill 350, and some shells fell on the ridge to the north of Valandovo. The order for the move to Tatarli or Calkali, as the two villages were adjacent, was as follows :—

Copy No. 2, 5th Connaught Rangers.

29th Infantry Brigade Order No. 4, by Brig.-General R. S. Vandeleur, C.M.G., commanding.

20.11.15.

Reference sheet Vodena—of 1 : 200,000 map.

In confirmation of verbal instructions issued to-day.

The Brigade will move as follows :—

I. Brigade H.Q. at 1200 to a point on the main road between Causli and Hasanli.

II. The 10th Hampshire Regt. at 1000 and the 5th Connaught Rangers at 10.30 independently to Tatarli.

III. The 30th Field Ambulance independently to Tatarli.

IV. The 10th Hampshire Regt. will detach two

Companies to relieve two Companies of the 6th Royal Munster Fusiliers on the Crête Simonet.

The officer in charge of these two Companies to report at the H.Q. of the 6th Munster Fusiliers at Tatarli, who will provide him with a guide to the positions to be occupied.

 Copy No. 1, 10th Hampshire Regt.
   No. 2, 5th Connaught Rangers.
   No. 3, 30th Field Ambulance.
   No. 4, Retained.

     (Sd.) T. G. ANDERSON, Major.
       B.M., 29th Brigade.

Orders at 0850.

After much delay, caused by the Ammunition Column cutting in in front of the Rangers on the only road or rather track to Tatarli, the Battalion reached its bivouacking ground in some rough ground north of the village at 1.20 p.m. Many of the Regiments that were about to proceed to take over the French lines were bivouacked in the small space available for the camp of the Battalion. These Battalions could not commence to move until the sun began to set. It was late when the men of the Rangers were able to pitch their own bivouacs. The Brigadier proceeded to Tatarli and then handed over the command of the two Regiments to Lieut.-Colonel Jourdain, who was ordered to consider his force as Divisional Reserve.

The Brigade Headquarters then moved back to near Hasanli.

All the villages in Serbia had been completely

cleared by the French, and all the inhabitants had been sent away. In this way Rabrovo, Valandovo, Tatarli, Calkali, Dedeli, Kajali, and Memisli were absolutely devoid of any inhabitants. A very necessary precaution.

Lieut.-Colonel Jourdain received a wire from Divisional Headquarters acquainting him that the force under his command was under the orders of the Division only, and that he was to take orders from them only.

The day broke with rain falling, but this cleared up later. The length of the march this day was 4½ miles only. Upon relief by the 30th and 31st Brigades, the French troops holding the line from the Kozlu Dere towards Kosturino began to file down by the woody track past Kajali to Tatarli, and there awaited orders from their own general.

Services by the chaplains were held as usual early on the 21st November, and afterwards orders were received from the Division to send out two officer's patrols towards Boluntili and Prstan.

Captain D. P. J. Kelly and 2nd Lieut. D. J. Cowan went out at 10 a.m. and rendered excellent reports, especially Captain Kelly, both of which were dispatched to Divisional Headquarters. Nothing could be seen of the Bulgarians round the right flank, which was then not wholly closed and secure.

Lieut. M. J. Fogarty with 80 other ranks joined the Battalion the same day from the Base. There were only a few registering shots by our guns to-day near Tatarli. At 9 a.m. on the 22nd, Brig.-General Nicol visited the Battalion at

Tatarli, and a large fatigue party of the Battalion were put to improve the roadway up to Kajali and Memisli.

There was a severe frost last night, and the men felt the cold in the rocky bivouac very keenly.

The night of the 23rd November was exceedingly cold, and there was again a severe frost.

The Battery near Tatarli opened on the Bulgarians, who were observed putting guns into position behind Hill 850, which was almost opposite the centre of the British line. Some sniping was heard later.

At 5 p.m. the Rangers, to the number of 100 men, pulled up a Battery nearly to the village of Kajali. Another fatigue party was furnished by the Battalion in repairing the ford over the Bojimi Dere near Rabrovo. This party was employed continuously day by day from 8 a.m. until sunset from this date, until the Battalion took over front-line trenches. Several Bulgarian prisoners were brought through the lines this day.

The night of the 23rd November and the morning of the 24th November were very cold indeed, and there was a very heavy frost. At 9 a.m. the enemy opened with shell-fire on the Batteries just east of the Battalion's bivouac, but after about two hours the shelling ceased with little loss.

The following night the Rangers (100) also helped to drag up another Battery of the 67th Brigade up the hill to near Memisli. This was very heavy fatigue work, but all men worked at it with cheerful willingness, and it was past 5 a.m. on the 25th before the work was completed. The night had been again excessively cold, and made sleep for many almost impossible, although in a more sheltered position than the men in the front line. Lieut.-General Sir B. Mahon and Brig.-General Nicol proceeded through Tatarli on the 28th November, and saw the men of the Battalion road-making near Kajali. The enemy, who were shelled by the British guns at 11.15 a.m. just east of Memisli, replied at 2.15 p.m. by shelling one of the Rangers' companies on the Kajali road, but without causing any casualties.

Eight Bulgarian prisoners were brought in to-day, two of whom were captured behind the Battery near Calkali.

As day broke on the 26th November rain and sleet began to fall, and later the downpour was very heavy. The tops of the hills were covered with snow, and the cold was very severe. The soldiers attempted to improve their bivouacs, but without much success. At 11.25 a.m. orders were sent to withdraw the two companies of the 10th Hants Regt. from the top of Crête Simonet. The cold was at this time very severe and the men were wet through, though very cheery, and quite saturated with rain, snow, and mud. There was, however, little sickness.

2nd Lieut. C. E. Gallwey was sent into Dojran this day to act as assistant to the D.A.D.O.S. at that station.

The heavy rain subsided towards evening, but at 4 a.m. on the 27th November snow began to

fall heavily, and this continued without intermission until 3 p.m.   When the snow ceased the
weather became intensely cold, and even the snow
which had fallen froze on the men's coats.   Where
the snow had melted, the pathway at once became
thick with ice, and the passage of baggage animals
with rations grew at the same time intensely
difficult.

The morning of the 28th November found the
Battalion still at Tatarli, encamped in a sea of
ice and mud, and little except their waterproof
sheets and blankets to protect them from the
severity of the weather.   The great-coats of the
soldiers were frozen quite stiff, and not until the
sun rose could they be rendered more pliable.

A patrol which had been sent out to get wood,
brought back two fully armed Bulgarians at
12.50 p.m. this day with over 250 rounds of
ammunition on each of them.

At about 5.45 p.m. on the 28th, the following
order was received from the 10th Division Headquarters :—

' 5th The Connaught Rangers.

' G. 136—28th—

' 30th Infantry Brigade will carry out following
reliefs to-morrow night.   Three Battalions in front
line will be relieved by Reserve Battalion and
5th Connaught Rangers and 10th Hampshire, who
will come under his orders when relief is complete.
The two Battalions 30th Infantry Brigade at
Tatarli will become Divisional Reserve under
orders of G.O.C. Division.   30th Infantry Brigade

1915   will notify 31st Infantry Brigade and 29th Infantry Brigade hour of relief. Addressed 30th Infantry Brigade, repeated 29th, 31st, 10th Hampshire, 5th Connaught Rangers. Acknowledge.

'10th Division, 1635.'

On the 29th November the following order was received from the 30th Infantry Brigade :—

' B.M. 5. 29th.

' The 10th Hampshire will relieve the 6th R.M.F. to-night and 5th Connaughts will relieve the 7th R.D.F. The 5th C. R.s will move from Tatarli in front of the 10th Hampshire.

' Guides from the relieved Bns. will meet the relieving Bns. at the mosque at Kajali at 1730.

' The 5th C. R.s will move off at 1615.

'(Sd.) P. VILLIERS-STUART, Maj.

1200.   ' B.M. 30th I.B.'

The Commanding Officer, Adjutant and Company Commanders were requested to proceed up to Kajali on the 29th November to meet representatives of the regiments they would relieve and to personally visit the trenches. This of course entailed a stiff climb of nearly three miles on a very slippery and rough road, while the cutting wind still further made progress somewhat slow. The Commanding Officer and other officers returned to the Battalion bivouac shortly before 1 p.m., and made arrangements to move up into position at 4.15 p.m. as ordered.

Brig.-General L. L. Nicol, who was at that time in temporary command of the 10th Division vice Lieut.-General Sir B. T. Mahon, commanding the Salonika Army, requested Lieut.-Colonel Jourdain to waive his right to command the 30th Brigade in view of his seniority to Lieut.-Colonel Cox, as he had been obliged to order the two Battalions of General Reserve up to give the 30th Brigade a spell of warmth at Tatarli.

General Nicol concluded by saying that ' it would add to the difficulties, if the command of the left section had to be changed ', and that he did not expect the Battalion (5th Connaught Rangers) would be more than 48 hours in the trench line or 72 at the most.

Lieut.-Colonel Jourdain, although senior in rank to Lieut.-Colonel Cox, accordingly was placed under the orders of that officer.

The Battalion paraded at a few minutes to four o'clock, and at 4.15 p.m. began to march up to the outpost line, but on arrival at the first height overlooking Tatarli, the companies waited for the sun to set, as parties of stretcher-bearers, bringing down men with frost-bitten hands and feet, had been heavily shelled by the enemy. The companies from this point onwards marched with intervals of 200 yards between them. At 5.5 p.m. the Battalion arrived at Kajali, and as each Company reached the mosque in the village, it was dispatched to its allotted position in the outpost line. Over 300 men had been sent down with frost-bite during the last two days from the front line.

2nd Lieut. A. C. Holmes reported sick this day and left the Battalion at Tatarli. The Battalion relieved the 7th Battalion Royal Dublin Fusiliers in the outpost line. The cold was intense, and the pathways up which all reliefs and baggage-mules with rations made their way to the outpost line were thick with eight inches of solid ice. It became consequently impossible to send up the morrow's rations by mules, and fatigue parties were required to carry up every article of bread, biscuit, groceries, meat and water during the night. After the severe climb from Tatarli and the onerous work of bringing up all provisions for the trenches, as well as their own blankets, coats and waterproof sheets, the men were very weary, but still the casualties from frost-bite were not numerous in the Rangers that night. The night was dark, and it was only a little before 11 p.m. that all the reliefs were completed.

The following night was intensely cold, and there was a very hard frost.

On the 30th November the Commanding Officer accompanied the acting Brigadier round the left section, including the 10th Hampshire Regt., the 5th Connaught Rangers, and the 7th Royal Munster Fusiliers and Cyclist Company in the order named. The trenches had been originally made by the French, and had not been improved since to any great extent.

It was on the 30th November possible to walk along the trench line without even being subjected to sniping from the enemy's lines. The officers and men of the Bulgarian Army were plainly seen some hundred yards away, carefully selecting machine-gun positions, and laying out trenches for their sharp-shooters, but no firing was indulged in by either of the combatants.

The 10th Hampshire Regt. had taken up the right of the 30th Brigade line, the 5th Connaught Rangers occupied the centre, and then the 7th Royal Munster Fusiliers and the Cyclist Company the extreme left. The Rangers, being somewhat stronger, took over the larger portion of the trench line in the centre. The work of improving the trench line began at once, on the afternoon of the 30th November, but the enemy interfered immediately, and sent several shells into any working party that showed themselves. It now became apparent that as long as no work on the line was in course of erection or completion, the enemy forbore expending either gun or rifle ammunition, but as soon as any work commenced, firing also commenced. The work of improving the trenches was both arduous and slow, as the supply of picks and shovels was limited and the sheets of ice on the bottom of the trenches made digging very hard. The sides of the trenches were frozen as hard as bricks, and as little work could be effectually done in the day-time, progress was slow. A Company, however, began an excellent communication trench which eventually was a source of great strength to the right of the Rangers' line. The day was cold but bright, and a severe frost again covered the country with a white cloak, and was responsible for several cases of frost-bite.

The practice, however, of making the men work at intervals during the night, and the provision of braziers in the trenches was responsible for the few cases of frost-bite in the Battalion.

The enemy subjected the Rangers' line to some sniping during the evening, and one shell fell into the fire trench, but there were no casualties.

On the 1st December the Bulgarians shelled A Company on the right for some time at 10 a.m., but the hostile guns ceased at 10.30 a.m.

Several of the enemy's working-parties were shelled, and the hostile guns began gradually to register the ranges of all the trench line. Heavy gun-fire from the French on the left of the Cyclist Company broke out at 1.20 p.m.

Lieut. R. Grove White, 7th Royal Dublin Fusiliers, who was commanding B Company, which was third from the right in the trench line, was severely wounded about 2.30 p.m., while superintending the improvement of the front line.

Considerable activity on the part of the enemy's snipers was apparent from this time until dark, and many shells from the Bulgarian guns fell near the trench line from 3 to 5 p.m.

Much labour was thrown on the companies hold-

ing the fire trenches, in having to carry up their
rations to the front.

D Company was at this time in reserve, with
one platoon in the front line on the left of B Company.   The position of the other companies ran :—

Bulgarian Trenches.

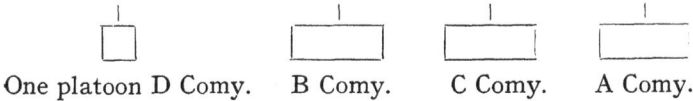

One platoon D Comy.   B Comy.   C Comy.   A Comy.

•
Headquarters.

Reserve, 3 Platoons D Comy.

At 9.20 a.m. on the 2nd December, confidential
instructions were given out at Brigade Headquarters to the Commanding Officer about a retirement, but no date for such a move was mentioned.
All kits were to be cut down to a minimum.   Inter-
mittent gun-fire went on nearly all day between the
opposing artillery and the British guns, and at
night a heavy discharge of ammunition took place
in the front, but no attack was made.

The lines now became a sea of mud and snow,
and the nights were oppressively cold and raw.
The men suffered severely.   Officers' valises for the
most part had been sent away down to Tatarli, and
all surplus kit of any kind was also dispatched to
the transport there, to be sent back to Salonika
via Dojran.

One man was accidentally shot this day and died
of his wounds on the following day.   Both officers
and men began to feel very keenly the continual

strain of outpost duty and the intense cold at night without adequate cover.

3rd December.   The morning broke with a damp cold mist overhanging the whole country.   The trenches were about a foot deep in water and slush, and could not be drained by any means.   In addition to this a continual look-out had to be kept throughout the whole trench line, as the enemy, under cover of the dense fog, could approach within a few yards of the trench line without being observed.   Patrols were accordingly sent out, but this only made the duty, already heavy, much heavier.   In one day forty-six men reported sick and many were sent down to hospital, some even in complete collapse from cold and inclement weather on the highlands of the Bulgarian frontier.   The snow was melting rapidly, but the whole bivouac was deep in mud and half-melted snow.   The trenches were in a deplorable condition.

The sound of heavy rifle and gun-fire reached the Rangers' lines soon after 9 a.m. from the left, held by the French, and this continued till after 2 p.m.

The work of improving the trench line was rapidly pushed on, but so badly sited were the trenches that little could be made of them.

On the 4th December the enemy began to shell the path leading to Kajali at 9.5 a.m., and soon afterwards heavy fire broke out in that part of the line held by the French. The sound of heavy gun-fire even from the direction of Krivolak was most pronounced. The enemy shelled the trench line at intervals during the morning, and at midday

began to shell Battalion Headquarters. The shells
fired to-day bore the name of Krupp on the shell-
cases, all the former shell-cases being marked with
the Buda Pesth mark, having been made for Bulgaria. At 1.30 p.m. the bombardment of the
Rangers' trench line grew heavier and more intense,
and parties of the enemy were apparent, assembling in the gully below Hill 850.

All men were quietly moved into the fire trenches
and stood to arms.

Parties of the enemy began to demonstrate
against the right of the Rangers' position, held by
A Company. A heavy fire was kept up on these
bodies of men, who were thus kept from achieving
anything from their demonstration.

The gun-fire on the trench line was particularly
deadly from the enemy's guns situated north-east
of Kosturino. These guns had during the previous
days registered the range to all the points of the
trench line occupied by the Rangers and the 10th
Hants especially. One man was brought down
severely wounded from D Company at 2.10 p.m.,
and several others who were wounded had to
remain in their trenches until sunset, as it was
impossible to remove them. The hostile gun-fire
was very persistent all the afternoon and did
not cease until nightfall (about 4.30 p.m.). The
Battalion stretcher-bearers then went up and
brought down all the wounded—six in number, and
carried them down to Kajali and Tatarli, a distance
of nearly four miles. All these men were severely
wounded, and had to be carried the whole way
down the hill during the night.

L

Patrols were pushed out at night, and the enemy did not attempt any further advance during the hours of darkness.

On the 5th December the day passed without incident, except that the enemy fired a few shells against the left of the Rangers' line at 10.30 a.m., but ceased almost at once.

Lieut. Tibbs reported that motor lorries were seen approaching from the direction of Strumnitza and disappearing behind Hills 800 and 850, north-east of Kosturino. Evidently motor wagons with ammunition. Some activity was also apparent in the front.

Divine Service was celebrated by the Chaplains for all men who could be spared from duty in the early morning. The day was fine and warm, and the snow had almost disappeared.

At 2 p.m. the Commanding Officer was summoned to the Headquarters of the 30th Brigade, where were assembled Brig.-General Nicol, Commanding 10th Division ; Brig.-General King-King, Commanding 31st Brigade, and Lieut.-Colonel Cox, Commanding 30th Brigade, with Lieut.-Colonel Leman, G.S.O. I, and the Brigade-Major 30th Brigade.

It was then explained to Lieut.-Colonel Jourdain that the retirement notified confidentially on the 2nd December would commence on the night of the 11th December, when the whole of the 30th Brigade would vacate the front line at about 10 p.m., and would take up a position in rear, which was not mentioned.

The line at present held by the 10th Hampshires,

the 5th Connaught Rangers, 7th Royal Munster 1915
Fusiliers, and the Company 7th Royal Dublin
Fusiliers holding 'Cyclists' Rest', would be occupied
on the night of the 11th December, when the 30th
Brigade had vacated same, by the Hampshire Regiment and Connaught Rangers only.   To facilitate
this, the ground occupied by the right Company of
the Hampshires at that time would be vacated
during the twenty-four hours in question (i. e. to
10 p.m. on the 12th December, when the Hampshire Regiment and Connaught Rangers would in
turn commence to vacate the front line).   This
latter space would have, however, to be patrolled
by the then right Company of the 10th Hampshires.

Later it was agreed to bring up the Cyclist Company to fill the gap at Cyclists' Rest.

The Connaught Rangers would thus occupy the
position from the left of the Hants, who would
move a little from the right to the left, and down
to the Cyclists' Rest.   This would have to be held
from the night (10 p.m.) of the 11th December to
10 p.m. on the 12th December.

The 10th Hampshires would then retire, followed
by the Rangers, and finally by the Cyclist Company.

The appended instructions, which had already
been acted upon, were issued to all concerned, and
were ordered to be carried into effect as soon as
possible.

10/D/No. 137 (A).

General. (*a*) All cooking will have to be done in
mess tins, but if possible twenty-four camp kettles

per Battalion will be retained to provide hot drink for the men.

(b) The 2nd blanket to be now withdrawn and returned from all troops except those who are occupying very exposed positions and who, in the opinion of G.O.C. Brigades, &c., must retain them until the last. No transport will in all probability be available for these. The numbers of blankets so retained to be wired to D.H.Q. by Brigades, &c., at 0900 to-morrow, 6th instant.

(c) Leather jerkins brought up by drafts must be withdrawn and returned to D.A.D.O.S., whose store is at Dojran Station, with vouchers showing numbers and units.

(d) All shoeing of animals to be put in good order forthwith, shoe-cases to be well filled with spare shoes and nails.

Q.M. Stores. To be practically all sent on ahead—a small supply of oil and flannelette to be carried in one of the S.A.A. carts.

Office Stores. Strictly limited to one small box per Battalion or office, and to Staff Officers' dispatch boxes.

Officers' Kits. The mess wagons being required for other purposes, mess stores cannot be carried. Officers' kits strictly limited both for Staff and Regimental Officers to a bundle not exceeding 15 lb. in weight. It may be possible to pick up stores at refilling points *en route*, but this cannot be guaranteed.

Transport. Instructions as to transport to be allotted will be issued later. The most necessary of the articles affected by the above orders are to be retained as long as supply wagons are running 1915 from the advanced dumps.

Due notice will be given as to this date.

(Sd.) D. SAPTE, Colonel.

A.A. & Q.M.G. 10th Division.

5th Dec. 1915.

The allotment of 1st Line limbered G.S. wagons per Infantry Battalion will be :—

Officers' kits, Battalion stores, Q.M. stores .	1
S.A.A.	5
Machine-guns	4
Battalion tools	2
Cooks' stores	1
Total	13

Lieut.-Colonel Jourdain was instructed at this Conference that he would be in command of the two Battalions 29th Brigade and the Cyclist Company from the night of the 11th December to the night of the 12th December, but the 31st Brigade would be on his right, and would retire over the hills in rear of that Brigade. The whole of Lieut.-Colonel Jourdain's force would retire by the Kajali–Rabrovo ravine on to Dedeli, but the whole force should be clear of the top of the Dedeli pass (Yellow House) by daylight on the 13th December. On arrival there this force could bivouac and thenceforth make its way towards Salonika by easy marches independently. It would not be required to do any further rearguard work, and would not be attached to any particular Brigade, until after arrival at Salonika. The eventual rearguard would be undertaken by the half-Brigade under Brig.-General Vandeleur, C.M.G., and the French. Such were the instructions given to Lieut.-Colonel Jourdain, commanding the Battalion.

As the Connaught Rangers and 10th Hampshires had been on continual trench duty since the 29th November (nearly 7 days instead of 72 hours), they were offered a relief by the 30th Brigade from the evening of the 6th December to the 10th December, when they would be required to take over the trench line, in order to allow the 30th Brigade to take up a position in rear.   Later it was explained that these two Regiments (Rangers and 10th Hampshires) would probably be brought up to the front on the 9th December.

Both Lieut.-Colonel Jourdain, speaking for the Rangers, and Major Beckett, who sent word for the 10th Hampshires, agreed to retain the trench line for the time between the 6th and 9th December. All the officers of the 5th Battalion preferred to remain in the front line rather than accept relief, which would necessitate a journey down to Tatarli, and a stiff climb back to their present trenches.

In the evening of the 5th December all stations were warned to be ready for an attack, as some Bulgarian prisoners had informed their captors that an attack was to have been made at 3 a.m. on the 3rd December, but had to be postponed on account of the fog.

At 10.20 p.m. the O.C. 7th Royal Munster Fusiliers reported that a patrol of Bulgars had run into one of their patrols, and that as soon as his observation posts had been withdrawn he was

going to fire 3 rounds independent fire into the
gully. This was done, but there was no response.

The remainder of the night passed without
incident, but at 7.15 a.m. on the 6th December
the enemy began to subject the fire trenches to
heavy sniping. A few minutes later the Bulgarian or German guns opened on the front
trench line, and especially on that part held by
the Rangers, which was easily enfiladed by the
hostile guns beyond Kosturino. The artillery
duel between the French on the left and the
hostile artillery was very incessant and sustained during the whole morning of the 6th
December. At 1.30 p.m. the enemy began to
shell B Company trenches on the left of the
Rangers' position.

At 2.30 p.m. enemy's fire from hostile guns
beyond Kosturino and behind Hill 850 literally
raked all the trenches from left to right, and
every trench was subjected to a severe enfilade
fire. This bombardment grew intense just before
3 p.m., and at the same time small bodies of the
enemy were observed coming down the hills in
front of the line and creeping into the dongas and
gullies below the front line.

At 3.25 p.m. A Company on the right was
closely engaged with the enemy, but was holding
its ground against the masses of the enemy who
were attempting to press forward. The whole
front line was soon after engaged, but the enemy
continued to shell the trenches with a heavy and
searching fire. At the same time one platoon of
D Company, which was in reserve, was sent up

to bring ammunition to, and to support A on the right of the line. This left only half D Company in reserve.

At 3.10 p.m. some of the French guns nearly behind the left of the British line began to shell the enemy on the hills west of Kosturino. These guns had hitherto been silent and their position had not been divulged.

The hostile artillery at 4 p.m. began to shell the second line and the Battalion headquarters, while the whole of the enemy's machine-guns and mountain guns shelled the first line, and the hostile infantry attempted to press forward, but the admirable behaviour of the men in the trench line effectually drove back the enemy to the gully below. The hostile fire was chiefly directed against the three companies holding the right centre of the position. Several hundreds of the enemy gradually crept down the slopes of Hill 850, and ensconced themselves in the gully below, keeping up a galling fire on the British fire trench. Many men were hit, but had to be kept in the fire trenches until after darkness fell, as it was impossible for them to be moved. At 5 p.m. the enemy's gun-fire grew slightly less, and soon broke out on what the enemy thought contained the reserves of the line. 2nd Lieuts. W. H. Sargaison and G. Robinson were buried by a shell, which completely blew in the whole parapet, killing Lieut. Sargaison, and wounding Lieut. Robinson. These two officers were most gallantly freed from the earth which covered them by Company Sergt.-Major O'Connor, Sergeant

McGarry, and Private Gallagher, of A Company.
From this time onwards, even throughout the
night, the hostile batteries beyond Kosturino
fired regular salvos along the ridge occupied by
the gallant Rangers, completely enfilading the
entire line of trenches.

At 5.14 p.m. the enemy commenced to demonstrate against the Rangers' front line, and exceedingly heavy rifle fire broke out along the
whole front. The enemy's guns which had been
brought down Hill 850 now came into play, and
actually blew in the trenches in several places.

As the light of day waned the noise of gun and
rifle fire grew intense and the enemy redoubled
his attempt to carry the line, but in vain. The
night, however, fell, and nowhere had the enemy
effected even a temporary lodgement.

Throughout the whole day the officers of these
companies ran back at periods through a perfect
hail of bullets to report progress to Battalion
headquarters.

The Bulgarians now sent up several star shells,
and at times attempted to draw the fire trenches,
to determine which trenches exactly were held
and in what strength. At times this fire was
returned, but orders were given to all Company
Commanders to reserve their fire as much as
possible. As soon as night fell, the wounded were
brought down as quickly as possible, rations
were sent into the trenches, and water-bottles were
replenished. To add to the difficulties of the
night, fresh meat was issued this night for the
first time for some weeks, and as no fires could

be lighted the meat was useless to all. The iron rations, which had been sorely needed, were brought up only the same evening, and were unable to be issued, as all available men were employed all night carrying up the day's rations into the trench line. Infantry fire did not cease until nearly 8 p.m., but at 9 p.m., 10.10 p.m., and 11.40 p.m., and on throughout the night, the enemy's guns raked the position from end to end, denying even rest to those who had fought hard throughout the day. The men, although subjected to very heavy shelling throughout the day, were in excellent spirits at night, and had inflicted loss on the enemy whenever possible.

Patrols which crept out when darkness set in reported that the Bulgarians had evidently retired altogether or had ensconced themselves in the gullies and water-courses which separated the combatants.

The work of all ranks on this day and during the ensuing night was beyond all praise. For every duty there were volunteers, and among those whose labours were almost continuous were Captain and Adjutant G. J. B. E. Massy, Lieut. J. I. O'Sullivan, R.A.M.C., and all the signalling staff and the stretcher-bearers. Few slept that night, and all men lay by their arms.

The early morning of the 7th December broke with a thick mist overhanging the whole country. At 6.20 a.m. the rocky eminence called Rocky Peak, just south of the village of Ormanli, which was held by a detachment of the Irish Fusiliers, was rushed and taken by the enemy. The cries of the Bulgarian infantry and the shrieks of those gallant defenders who remained until overwhelmed and who paid the price of their devotion, could be plainly heard from the Rangers' position.

The possession of this rocky hill was to affect the position of the remainder of the line, as the enemy could now bring machine-guns to enfilade the trench line both to their right and left.

At 6.50 a.m. the enemy again opened on the Rangers' trench line with artillery from all their batteries both beyond Kosturino and beyond Hill 850. The fog still clung to the countryside, and even at 7 a.m. showed no sign of lifting.

At 7.10 a.m. the rattle of rifle fire resounded all along the front, and the enemy attempted to press forward but was unable to do so.

At 8.5 a.m. the hostile guns, which had been brought up the gully to behind the 'Hill of Howth', an eminence facing the left centre of the Rangers' position, and only about 650 yards from the fire trenches, began to shell the trenches, and this fire was both heavy and concentrated. This was especially directed against the four machine-guns, which were doing good service. The trenches were in many places blown right in.

The previous night, scouts sent forward had reported many dead bodies of the enemy near Hill of Howth. At this point (9 a.m.) the enemy attempted to press forward covered by machine and heavy guns. Their machine-gun batteries on Rocky Peak began to annoy the defenders of the line, and large bodies of the enemy were observed massing at the bottom of Hill 850.

The steady and well-directed fire of the defenders broke up every advance, and many of the enemy were seen to fall. This went on without the slightest intermission until 11.25 a.m.

The French position overlooking the Strumnitza road was also being heavily shelled, but was splendidly held. The British artillery, although requested continually to search the gully below the Hill of Howth and 850, were quite unable to do so, and their fire was never effective. The majority of the shells went too high, or went completely over the enemy.

The enemy's batteries beyond Kosturino were perfectly deadly and were able to outrange any of the British artillery. These shells were always marked with the Krupp mark, showing that the artillery was mostly armed with German guns, if not actually German.

The enemy had been reported massing at 9.50 a.m., and were almost completely hidden from view, although only some 600–700 yards from the fire trenches. Such was the state of the front-line trenches.

The battle went on all the morning, and not for a moment did the sound of rifle fire die down.

At 1.30 p.m. one machine-gun was knocked out of action by a direct hit, and soon after another one had the barrel casing pierced and rendered useless.

At 1.40 p.m. large reinforcements were seen approaching, and huge masses of the Bulgarian infantry were reported massing in all the valleys and gullies along the front. The artillery fire on the British side had almost died down and was most ineffective. Every available man was at his post, with the exception of one platoon, which had been on incessant fatigue, and there were no reserves. One Company of the 7th Royal Dublin Fusiliers, which had been placed at the service of Lieut.-Colonel Jourdain at 8 p.m. on the 6th December, had been withdrawn at 6.25 a.m. on the 7th December without previous notice, except a message from the Officer in command, saying that he was moving off. Captain R. R. Martin with 35 men from Base details had joined on the evening of the 6th December, and these had at once been utilized.

At 2 p.m. the enemy was reported boldly advancing over the Hill of Howth, but the men in the trenches, although under a merciless fire from all quarters, steadfastly maintained their position, and kept down the advancing infantry. The enemy were simply mown down by the Rangers' fire. Along the whole front the noise of the rifle fire and machine-guns was appalling. The enemy began to surge forward, but although the hostile machine-gun fire was both incessant and very deadly, they were able to make little ground.

The enemy now directed their artillery to search the ravines and valleys behind the fire trench, and shell after shell fell shrieking even down the Kajali–Rabrovo ravine. Not an inch of ground was free from the hostile batteries.

Soon after 2 p.m. B Company on Dollymount became closely engaged with the enemy, and,

1915   although sorely pressed, maintained their position against the huge masses of hostile infantry that surged up the broken slope directly in front of them. Numbers of the enemy were mown down by the steady fire of the defenders, but they still pressed on.

The artillery on the enemy's side redoubled their efforts, and shell after shell fell almost into the trenches, and then the range being suddenly increased, shell after shell fell into the ravine, where the stretcher-bearers were unselfishly doing their extremely thankless but dangerous duty. All the enemy's machine-guns seemed to break silence, and after a perfect hail of bullets had swept the line of the fire trenches, the Bulgarian infantry boldly stood up and advanced towards the trenches. There were at this time over 5,000 of the enemy massed below the position held by B and C Companies, more on the right strongly opposed A Company, while parties of the enemy, who had got into some trenches on the right of that Company, practically enfiladed them, but under Capt. Kelly they gallantly stood their ground.

The instant the hostile forces commenced to advance in close formation the occupants of the trenches stood up and poured their fire into the masses of the enemy. Many were observed to fall, and the losses of the enemy must have been heavy, but they still came on. At 2.30 p.m. the masses of the enemy simply poured over the trenches, bayoneting all those who still sought to bar their advance, and shooting the wounded without mercy.

The line at Dollymount (Hill 400) was taken, but
A Company held on tenaciously on the right,
although the trenches on their right and the
majority of those on their left were in occupation
of the enemy.

The position of C Company had become critical
directly they were enfiladed by the Bulgarians, and
many were here bayoneted by the enemy. The
platoon of D Company fell back fighting, and, after
a protracted resistance, A Company fell back only
when the enemy had got round his flanks, so as
to make retreat almost hopeless.

The report that the line had been broken was
sent in to the Headquarters of the Brigade at
2.45 p.m., and the inrush of the Bulgarian infantry
took place at 2.30 p.m. The most strenuous and
gallant resistance was made by all these companies,
and even when nearly surrounded the greater part
of A Company still held on to their position.

The enemy almost at once began to shoot those
who resisted, and bayoneted even those lying
wounded in the trenches or behind the trench line.

The survivors who gradually made their way
down the rugged hill-side were subjected to a dropping fire from the enemy above, and they were
mercilessly mown down by the shrapnel and rifle
fire of the enemy. Many, however, grievously
wounded, rejoined the Battalion and proceeded
with Headquarters which moved down the Kajali–
Rabrovo ravine, where the men of many regiments
were already marching towards Dedeli.

The majority of the survivors of A Company,
under Captain Kelly, twenty-six in number, fought

their way back to Crête Simonet and attached themselves to the part of the 30th Brigade which had come up and had taken up a position on that hill, and who rejoined the Battalion early the next day. At 3.2 p.m. the Battalion Headquarters, situated behind the centre of the line, was vacated, and the remnants of the Battalion, pursued by the shrapnel of the enemy, marched down the ravine, where the men of B, C, and D Companies, with some of A, were assembling.

It was now found quite impossible to take up any position on the Crête Rivet, as the sides were almost precipitous, and there was no approach from the Kajali–Rabrovo ravine.

The troops on the right of the line had retired in the direction of Kajali, pursued by the gun-fire of the Bulgarians.

In the ravine the Rangers were collected, and here 324 of the Battalion—41 of the 10th Hampshire Regiment, 56 of the 7th Royal Dublin Fusiliers, as well as strong parties of the 7th Royal Munster Fusiliers, were fallen in, and at 5.35 p.m. were marched to the entrance of the Dedeli defile, which was reached at 7.5 p.m. Many of the men were very severely wounded and were brought away by their comrades, or by a limber, which was requisitioned for that purpose. Very few men had any ammunition beyond a few rounds, and few had had any food whatever since the previous evening. The behaviour of these gallant men was excellent, and many men had even gaping wounds, having marched unassisted from the trench line.

The G.O.C. 10th Division ordered Lieut.-Colonel

Jourdain to bring the Battalion near the Divisional 1915
Headquarters at Dedeli, and at the same time sent
for the first line transport, which at that time was
near Tatarli, in order that rations might be served
out to the men.

The men were bivouacked near Dedeli, and
during the night some few men were collected,
who came in later. The Detachments of the 10th
Hampshires and 7th Royal Dublin Fusiliers rejoined their units the next day. The ammunition
in the possession of the transport was served out to
those men who required it, and rations were drawn
for and distributed to the men of all units with
the Battalion. The Rangers remained for the
night of the 7th December at Dedeli.

The men had gallantly held the whole trench
line for two days in spite of the masses of the
enemy, who endeavoured several times to push
forward under cover of their gun and machine-gun
fire, and until the moment when the enemy rose
and boldly advanced for the last 100 yards on the
trench line—unprotected except for two strands of
wire—the defenders reserved their fire, except for
conspicuous targets, as ammunition could not be
wasted. At that moment the men of the Battalion
poured their fire into the serried masses of the
enemy, and the losses must have been terrific.
The enemy then surged forward, and swept the line
literally from the trenches and the survivors over
the ridge beyond. No men left the trenches until
the enemy passed the line, and with six officers out
of nine fallen, they fought on to the last, and when
the remnants were formed up in the ravine behind

M

the lines, many were found to be wounded, although they did not report their wounds on parade. Even after arrival at Salonika, several men were discovered who had up to then not reported their wounds received on the 7th December.

When the line had been pierced the enemy sent his shells into the bivouac of the Reserve Battalion, and then after that followed the survivors until darkness fell. During the actions of the 6th and 7th December, no men reported sick and no men were sent down from the Battalion except those who had been wounded. All men of the Rangers retired with the Battalion except those who made their way back under Captain Kelly, and fought the next day on the Crête Simonet. The stand of the right of the line, even after their right flank was turned, did them much credit.

The following information, which was rendered to the Brigade, is republished here :—

'Upon taking over the trenches held by the 7th Battalion Royal Dublin Fusiliers, the whole line was covered with a thick coating of snow, which had been frozen hard, especially in the neighbourhood of the trenches, where the snow had melted and become frozen. Digging was exceedingly hard, and little could at first be done to improve the trenches.

'When the snow began to melt, the trenches began to fill with icy cold water, and nearly the whole of the line had to stand in water during the daytime. At night, the men were ordered to move about noiselessly behind the trench, but to avoid giving away their position : as there was no moon, and often a thick mist, this was quite practicable.   When the work of improving the trenches became more possible, the enemy began to snipe and harass the workers, and the three communication trenches were dug by order under a dropping fire by daylight, and only when night fell could this be continued with any security at all.   The trenches were made much more secure by the morning of the 6th December, and it was mainly to this improvement that the men of the Battalion were able to hold the enemy at bay until the afternoon of the 7th December.

' It was a fact that the exact line had become well known to the enemy before the line was taken over by the Battalion by the display of blankets, &c., outside the trenches by day, and by fires in the trench line at night.

' The occasional shelling by the enemy was solely for the purpose of range-taking, and before the 4th December nearly all shells fell not near men who showed themselves, but in the actual trenches. The "dugouts" behind the ridge were of no protection, as they could be easily enfiladed, and it was not possible in the position to lay out better ones.

' Tools were scarce, and had to be kept in continual use in the fire trenches and in making communication trenches, of which there were none before the arrival of the Battalion.

' The bringing up of rations was from the beginning a very great drawback, as all rations had at first to be man-handled from the mosque at Kajali to the trenches.   This meant great labour for all the men in the front trenches.   When the snow

1915 and ice had melted, the men could not be spared from the trenches for this purpose. The three platoons in reserve were employed on this service, and fatigue work was very constant for this party.

'A Company made a very good communication trench between the first line and the "dugouts" behind, and to this may be attributed the success of this Company to maintain its position after the rest of the line had been rushed, aided of course by the fine work put in by Captain Kelly.

'The enemy machine-guns were concealed in the rugged sides of the Hill 850, and the broken formations at the side of and below the same hill.

'The machine-guns of the Battalion, although carefully handled, had to be placed in the trench line, and were a sure target for the enemy's guns. Most gallant behaviour was shown by Sergeant McGarry and Company Sergt.-Major O'Connor in digging out a dead and a wounded officer under severe machine-gun fire. The equipment of the former, which he had taken off during the operation, was literally cut to pieces by machine-gun fire. The enemy had managed to draw the fire of

the trench line on one dark night, and the intervals
which had been left in the fire trench were consequently apparent to them. This was of great
service in the closing stages of the attack.

' The fire of the artillery never seemed to domi-
nate or even to keep down that of the enemy. It
was found impossible to search the gullies in front
of the position by artillery fire.

After
several nights of incessant night duty in the
trenches, the officers and all the men behaved
splendidly. There were only nine officers on duty
in the trenches, and night duty became very frequent. Their work was done splendidly, and when
Lieut. Grove White was wounded on the 1st
December, and 2nd Lieut. Sargaison killed on the
6th December at the same time 2nd Lieut. G.
Robinson was blown up and wounded, besides
being severely shaken, the strain became very
great.

' Four officers were reported missing, and of
these one has since been reported as wounded and
a prisoner, and three killed. Three officers escaped

1915 from among the hordes of Bulgarian infantry and rejoined the Battalion.

'The loss of the Rocky Peak was considerable, as it enabled the enemy to bring an enfilade machine-gun fire on the right of the trench line, and made the defence still more difficult. When the enemy ascertained the exact range of the communication trenches, all reports had to be sent back over the open ridge to the telephone operator, and much gallantry was shown by officers and others on this service. Every movement of the enemy was at once transmitted to the Headquarters 30th Brigade without delay. The system of deep gullies in the front of the Rangers' line was particularly favourable to the enemy, and concealed his dispositions admirably. A Company, although forced to leave the first line twice, returned and successfully held on for nearly an hour, but eventually retired by 5 Tree Hill on to Crête Simonet, rejoining the Battalion the next day. No man left the trenches until absolutely driven thence by the enemy, and one party under Sergeant Holmes was actually brought back by Captain Kelly and Corporal Nolan, who had shown splendid service, to trenches which had been taken by the enemy.

'When retirement became a necessity, all the officers remained to the last, and in the case of the three officers who rejoined, they were the very last to leave the line. The men, when called upon to form up in the ravine just behind the position, did so at once, and all details of other regiments showed a willingness to obey the orders of the O.C. 5th Connaught Rangers. When it is taken into consideration that not one officer, except the Adjutant and the Officer Commanding, had even one and a half years' service, their performance is most gallant and beyond praise. The C.O. regrets the loss of some promising officers, who gallantly remained at their posts and paid the penalty for their devotion to duty.

' The signallers both in the trenches and in the Headquarter section all remained at their posts until given permission to leave. Their work was quite excellent. They performed most useful and necessary work with an endurance thoroughly praiseworthy.

' The work of the stretcher-bearers was worthy of great commendation.

' I desire to specially mention the names of the following officers :—

' Temp.-Captain D. P. J. Kelly.

' 2nd Lieut. G. Robinson (wounded).

' 2nd Lieut. D. J. Cowan (wounded and missing).

' 2nd Lieut. H. H. L. Richards (missing, afterwards reported killed).

' Lieut. M. J. Fogarty.

' 2nd Lieut. F. W. Illingworth (Scot. Rifles, attached).

' 2nd Lieut. W. H. Sargaison (killed).

' The enemy were seen to shoot and bayonet the wounded, and those who were no longer able to wage an equal combat.

' I regret that the losses are very severe, but I am of opinion that the position could not have been possibly held longer, and that if ample reserves had been available on the 7th December, the line might have been recovered for a short time, but the vastly predominating amount of the hostile artillery made the line from near Kosturino to the Serbian Border House quite untenable.

' The final assault was carried out by more than five regiments of infantry, who pierced the middle of the line, and over 5,000 men were launched against B and C Companies alone. There were many more regiments in reserve and below Hill 850, and also behind the line of hills held by the enemy.

' The losses of the enemy were severe, and many men were seen to fall in the final assault.'

On the 21st December 1915, the names of the following officers and men of the 5th Battalion the Connaught Rangers were submitted for good service during the actions of the 6th and 7th December 1915 :—

'*Officers.*—Lieut. and Temp.-Captain D. P. J. Kelly, 5th Battalion the Connaught Rangers, for gallant service on the 6th and 7th December, when commanding the right Company, when he held his position although the Company on his left had been driven in by the enemy, who were in overwhelming force.

' Lieut. M. J. Fogarty, for good service on the 6th and 7th December, when commanding C Company until his Company was rushed by vastly superior forces of the enemy.

' 2nd Lieut. G. Robinson, for great gallantry on the 6th December, when, although wounded by a shell, and having been completely buried by the explosion of same, continued to assist in the

defence, and did not desist until ordered to leave
the firing line. This officer was a splendid example
to the men, and I would like to especially bring
forward his services for great gallantry.

'No. 3,660, Sergeant J. McGarry, for gallant and
good service on the 6th December, when at great
personal risk, and under a heavy machine-gun fire,
he dug out 2nd Lieuts. Robinson and Sargaison,
both of whom had been buried by having the
trench blown in by a high explosive shell, also for
continuous good work and gallant conduct in
directing fire, and in directing the defence during
the two days' action. I cannot too highly recommend this N.C.O.

'No. 10,103, Acting Company Sergt.-Major William O'Connor, for most gallant and signal service
in assisting to dig out two officers under heavy
machine-gun fire, and for most gallant service on
the 6th and 7th December, in directing fire and in
conducting the defence after the trenches near by
had been rushed.

'No. 3,918, Sergeant Daniel Flynn, and No.
10,020, Corporal Robert William Halpin (both reported missing), for most gallant and signal service
with machine-guns, which they used with most
splendid tenacity and did not desist until every
round was expended, and the trench had been
rushed by the enemy. These two N.C.O.s' work
was beyond praise.

'No. 5,582, Private J. Folan, for conspicuous
gallantry on the 6th and 7th December, when in

command of a trench, and although wounded, he still conducted the defence and maintained his trench after the line had been rushed by the enemy.

' No. 9,299, Corporal J. Stewart, for most conspicuous gallantry, when with No. 1,035, Lance-Corporal Francis Ormonde, after all the occupants of the trench had been killed and wounded, they remained and kept up a deadly fire on the enemy, and inflicted heavy loss on the hostile infantry.

' Nos. 9,103, Private William Martin, and 5,034, Private M. McDonnell, for gallant service, in face of a heavy machine-gun fire and heavy shelling, they advanced and bombed the enemy out of a piece of dead ground in front of the trenches on the 7th December.

' No. 3,381, Lance-Corporal Thomas Stevens, for gallant service in acting as observer under a heavy fire during the whole of the 7th December, even when the enemy's fire was exceedingly heavy.

' No. 3,707, Lance-Corporal F. Ball, for good service, when in charge of the signal station, in going out several times under a heavy fire to mend the line, which had been cut by shell fire.   This he did several times.

' No. 10,363, Private J. McLean, and No. 254, J. Smithers, for gallant and good service in carrying messages under a heavy fire on several occasions.

' I am of opinion that there were many cases which I have overlooked, but which I am unable to recommend owing to insufficient evidence.

I should, however, like to bring to notice the gallant behaviour of the following :—

'2nd Lieut. D. J. Cowan (missing and wounded).

'2nd Lieut. H. H. L. Richards (missing).

'No. 1,034, Corporal John Nolan.

Who highly distinguished themselves on the 6th and 7th December, and who stayed at their posts in a most gallant way and are now reported missing. I cannot speak too highly of their services. Corporal Nolan's work was beyond praise.

'Capt. G. J. B. E. Massy (Adjutant) and Lieut. H. C. Bell (signal officer) also performed most excellent service on the dates mentioned.'

The *Peninsula Press* dated 20th December, 1915, contains the following :—

Serbian Front. After the retirement of the Serbian Army into Albania, and the hostile occupation of Monastir, it was clear that the positions of the Allies in Serbia must become untenable in view of the strength which the Bulgarians would be able to concentrate against them. The Bulgarians' attacks appear to have culminated about the 10th or 11th.

The retirement was carried out deliberately, the railway bridges and tunnels were blown up as they were left behind, and the Allied force has now for several days not been molested by the Bulgarians. A War Office communiqué contains the following :—

' After violent attacks of the enemy in overwhelming numbers, the 10th Division, with the help of reinforcements, succeeded in retiring to a strong

1915 position from Lake Doiran westwards towards the Vardar Valley in connexion with Allied Divisions. It is reported that they fought well against the heaviest odds, and it was largely due to the gallantry of the troops, especially the Munsters, Dublins, and Connaught Rangers, that the withdrawal was successfully accomplished. Owing to the mountainous nature of the country it was necessary to place eight field guns in a position from which it was impossible to withdraw them when the retirement was effected. Our casualties numbered about 1,300.'

The Bulgarian forces attacking the British Force were stated to have been composed of two Divisions (*Temps* correspondent at Salonika).

The *Giornale d'Italia* of 10th December stated that at least one German Division (about 20,000 men) was already in action between Valandovo and Dojran.

The correspondents agree that the British contingent was specially marked for the German attack, but they also asserted that the British artillery was proving surprisingly effective.

The *Petit Parisien* published the following telegram :—' The eventuality which my last telegrams foreshadowed took place yesterday, when the Bulgarians in strong force, and probably supported by German artillery, made a very violent attack on the British left wing in the sector extending from Rabrovo to Kosturino, Ormanli and Memisli. This, unfortunately, is the beginning of what has been expected for the last few days. In view of the strength of the forces brought against us, we cannot offer an effective resistance in the present position.'

The Times of 10th December published the following War Office communiqué :—

' On 6th December the Bulgarians, after a heavy bombardment, attacked our troops to the west of Lake Doiran.

' Our advanced trenches were entered by small parties of Bulgarians, who were immediately driven out with the bayonet.

' On the morning of the 7th the Bulgarians attacked again, and by weight of superior numbers drove our troops out of their position. Under cover of darkness the troops were withdrawn to a new line. Reports as to our losses have not yet been received. On the 8th, the British troops successfully repulsed all attacks, and in the evening they were withdrawn to a new position in order to conform with the general alinement.'

' The Bulgarian Base is Ishtip, whence large forces have been sent to Strumnitza. From this point violent attacks have been directed against Kosturino, on the front held by the British, who are hastily entrenching on the Bogovitch heights, north of Doiran. A telegram to the Hestia says that the attack continues and that the Bulgarian object appears to be to pierce the British line in order to seize Strumnitza Station.

' Under date of the 8th, Reuter's correspondent telegraphs that the Bulgarian attacks during the last two or three days appear to have been somewhat more serious than originally reported. In the matter of artillery the Bulgarians are apparently adopting the German tactics of deluging their objective with shell-fire before attempting an infantry advance. Since Sunday the British lines have engaged the principal share of their attention, and before the superior strength of the enemy our outposts, which had been pushed ahead of our positions for tactical purposes, have been gradually falling back to our main lines.

'Some hand-to-hand fighting has actually taken place, the Bulgarians having crossed bayonets with a party of the Connaught Rangers, who made short work of their opponents, driving them from the trench which they had occupied under cover of artillery' (*Times*, 10th December).

The same paper stated on the 8th December :—

'The surmise that the Bulgarian demonstration against our positions might develop into a very serious offensive is being justified by their subsequent action, which has consisted in a series of fierce assaults, supported by artillery, directed by day and by night against our right wing from Demir Kapu to Kosturino.

'These have so far been successively beaten off, but the enemy is continually being reinforced and apparently intends to renew his attacks with fresh troops with the object of gaining Strumnitza Station, towards which the German cavalry, mentioned in my previous dispatch, has been making reconnaissances. Prisoners taken by the French in these engagements affirm that the majority of the officers of the attacking forces are Germans.'

Many officers and N.C.O.s wearing German uniforms were seen by the 7th Royal Munster Fusiliers and the left of the Connaught Rangers in the actions of the 6th and 7th December.

The Commander of the 30th Brigade on the evening of the 6th December informed Lieut.-

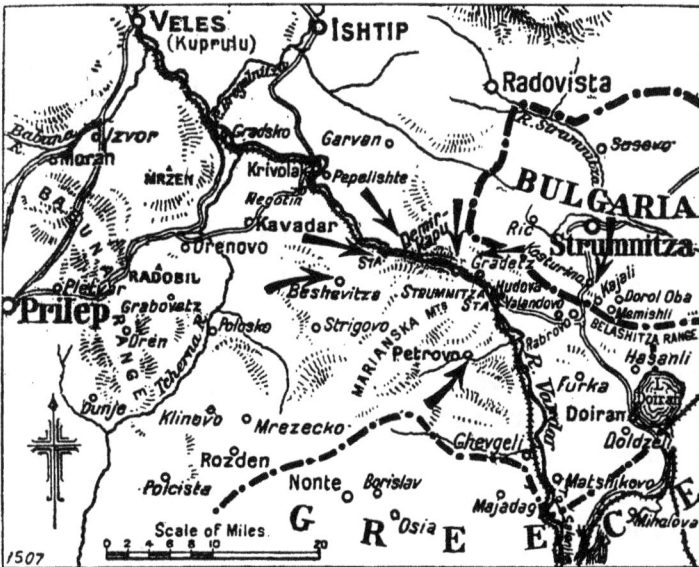

Reproduced from *The Times*, by kind permission.

Colonel Jourdain that the Battalion had fought splendidly on that day, and that from the Brigade Headquarters it seemed hardly possible that a human being could live on the ridge occupied by the Rangers, during the bombardment of that afternoon.

The following message signed 'Priority', but timed 1420 (i. e. 2.20 p.m.), was received at Battalion Headquarters at 2.45 p.m. on the

1915 7th December, after the centre of the line had been penetrated :—

'O.C. 5th Connaught Rangers.

'B.M. 1.—7th December.

'In the event of a general retreat being ordered, the Reserve Battalion (7th R.D.F.) will take up a position on Crête Rivet at once to cover the retirement of rest of Brigade AAA. The 10th Hampshire Regt. will retire by right of 7th Dublins on to Crête Simonet, first occupying 5 Tree Hill to cover their retirement and that of 5th C.R.s A.A.A.

'The 5th Connaught Rangers will retire across the NW. slope of 5 Tree Ridge and eventually by the left of 7th R.D.F. on Crête Rivet to the NW. slope of Crête Simonet, AAA. The 7th Dublins on Cyclists' Rest and 7th R.M.F. will retire by the Kajali–Rabrovo ravine, and will concentrate at the junction of Rabrovo–Tatarli road and point at which short cut from the ravine to Dedeli meets it, AAA.

'30th Brigade,
'14. 20.'

At the time of the receipt of the message, the right of the line of the 30th Brigade had been driven in, and consequently 5 Tree Hill was not occupied by any troops, nor could it have been manned by the British, as the enemy were already in occupation of the heights which commanded it. The officer belonging to the Battalion (2nd Lieut. D. J. Cowan), who had three days previously reconnoitred the route by which the Battalion would retire on the 12th December, was wounded and a prisoner in the hands of the enemy, and the route by which the Battalion should retire was unknown. It was found quite impossible to scale the heights of Crête Rivet from the ravine, and if any of the Battalion had scaled the cliffs from the ravine, they could not have retired from that position without coming down again the same way as they ascended. There was a huge cleft in the range, over 100 feet deep, which barred the communication between the front nearest the enemy and the southern part of Crête Simonet. The second in command of the 6th Royal Dublin Fusiliers corroborates this statement, and states that on the 8th December, the Company of his Regiment which held the advanced position was cut off and captured, there being no possible line of retreat for them.

The officer in command reported to the 10th Divisional Headquarters that he was assembling the Battalion in the ravine, and later a verbal message was sent out for the Battalion to move on Dedeli, which was done, and the remnant of the Rangers reached the bottom of the pass soon after 7 p.m.

At the Divisional Headquarters Brig.-General Nicol informed the O.C. that the Battalion would remain in bivouac there that night, and that he would try and procure ammunition and rations, as the men had practically none left.

Nearly all the men's great-coats and blankets had been lost, besides all the company stores and documents, which had been in the support line, and

N

could not be brought away in time. There was little sleep that night for many, as the intense cold prohibited even those who were worn out with continuous duty for the last nine days.

A thick mist, very damp and penetrating, covered the country, and drenched those without coats, who had absolutely no cover from the weather but their equipment.

On the morning of the 8th December, the Battalion was ordered to remain where it was, and rations were later obtained in small quantities for the men.

Many of the men were in truth without equipment and any covering whatever, and some few had lost their serge frocks.

Later the Battalion furnished a party to erect barbed wire entanglements at the bottom of the defile.

Brig.-General Nicol came to see the Battalion at 12.40 p.m., and said the 31st Brigade were being heavily attacked on the right. At 12.50 the Battalion was ordered to move as soon as possible to the south end of the Kajali ravine, which it did in 15 minutes, leaving those sick, wounded, or unable to march at Dedeli.

The Rangers reached the end of the ravine at 2.20 p.m. and relieved the 7th Royal Munster Fusiliers at 3 p.m., who moved towards Tatarli.

The Officer Commanding 7th R.M.F. informed the O.C. Rangers that the look-out post on the top of the hill reported that the French troops and the 6th Royal Dublin Fusiliers were retiring rapidly, and that the Bulgarians were even then within 1,000 yards of the southern crest, i.e. near the defile or near the Rangers' position.

The line was at once drawn back from under the range of hills, and was situated on the southern bank of the Kozlu Dere with a good field of fire towards the range of hills in front. One Company was entrenched near the French on a hill near the Kajali–Rabrovo ravine.

Trenches were at once dug with the available entrenching implements, and the outpost line had only just been pushed out, when a mounted officer rode to the Battalion Headquarters at 4.15 p.m. and ordered the Battalion to retire at once on Dedeli again. This was followed by another message a few minutes afterwards, and the Battalion marched at once towards the bottom of the pass at Dedeli. This was reached at 5.25 p.m., and on reporting to 10th Division Headquarters, the officer commanding was instructed to report to Lieut.-Colonel Fair, R.E., and to remain to hold the Dedeli pass. All available men were placed in position, mostly at the bottom of the pass, with the Cyclist Company, or working under the Royal Engineers.

Soon after other corps began to arrive from the front, and marched up the defile towards the Yellow House, which was at the top of the pass. The night was again very raw and cold, and officers and men, with their clothing and boots saturated with the damp, felt the cold keenly.

No blankets or great-coats were available, and the troops bore these privations without a murmur, and were in fact exceedingly cheerful.

The sight of these men, harassed and sleepless, was enough to draw pity from the sternest heart, and the officers were also under the same disadvantages and behaved admirably throughout these trying times. The Battalion had marched six miles this day.

The Headquarters of the Battalion was at the village of Dedeli.

The Battalion paraded at 5 a.m. on the 9th December, and marched off in the dark and misty morning a few minutes afterwards up the pass. A party of the Battalion had been left at the bottom of the pass with the Cyclists, to help to defend the entrance and to prepare obstacles. The French had retired off Hill 350, and the whole road was simply blocked with French transport and guns, and progress was almost impossible up the narrow road. However, after almost endless struggling, the Rangers got ahead of this long line of vehicles of all kinds, and marched on until they met the 7th Royal Munster Fusiliers, about a quarter of a mile from the head of the pass. The Battalion was here halted and some posts were put out by Colonel Fair, on both sides of the road. The men prepared breakfast, and at 9.5 a.m. the remainder of the Battalion marched on up the pass and halted again at 10.30 a.m. on some ground near the Yellow House. Here the few remaining men of the Battalion were ordered to dig some small trenches to command the head of the pass. The sound of musketry and gun fire still resounded from the direction of Cestovo, which was occupied by the French. The night had been terribly cold, and the day was also both

raw and sunless. Brig.-General Vandeleur, C.M.G.,
Colonel Herbert, Lieut.-Colonel Cox, and Lieut.-
Colonel Fair, R.E., commanded sections of the
defence, and the Rangers were placed under
Lieut.-Colonel Fair, R.E., who held the Dedeli
defile, which was adjoining the French right.

The Dedeli defile had one rather narrow road
with the cliff overhanging on one side, and the
river bed below on the other side. Several wagons
of the French had in the dark and misty night
gone completely over into the torrent bed, and
were smashed to pieces below. The losses in the
regiments near Kajali and Kosturino were reported
to be as follows :—

6th Royal Dublin Fusiliers, 170, other ranks.

7th Royal Dublin Fusiliers, 100, including one
officer.

7th Royal Munster Fusiliers, about 150 casualties
in all.

The casualties in the Rangers were as follows :—

Officers killed	1
Officers wounded	2
Officers missing (afterwards reported three killed, and one wounded and a prisoner)	4
Officers sick to Hospital . . .	4
Other ranks killed	31
Other ranks wounded . . .	120
Other ranks wounded and missing .	38
Other ranks missing	179
Other ranks sick to Hospital . .	144
Including officers—Total	523

Strength leaving Salonika . . .	983
Arrived 21.11.15	60
Arrived 21.11.15	18
Arrived Kajali	35
Total	1,096

* Total at Salonika on return, including
      all rejoined, &c., on 18.12.15 . 584

A Company lost heavier than the other companies, their position being very exposed, and their
defence was well maintained until over 50 per cent.
of the defenders had fallen. The batteries which
had been brought up the defile and were now in
position near the top of the pass opened fire for
ranging at 2.45 p.m. on the 9th December, but
only fired several rounds.

At night, C Company, under Captain R. R. Martin, proceeded down to the bottom of the pass to
form a support to the outpost line there. Many
French troops passed the Rangers' bivouac by the
roadside both going up and down the pass. All
the bridges were being mined and were to be
blown up when all the troops had passed.

On the 10th December the weather still continued very cold, and the men suffered very much
from the intense cold at night with no covering of
any kind. There was, however, little sickness, and
the behaviour and cheerfulness of the men were
beyond all praise. Heavy rifle fire was heard all the
morning, and was especially heavy on the left at

* Regimental transport, officers' chargers and grooms, and
Quartermaster's stores were at Tatarli while the Battalion
occupied the trench line.

2 p.m.   The 7th R.M. Fusiliers were ordered down to the bottom of the pass at 2.30 p.m.   At 2.30 p.m. Lieut.-General Sir B. T. Mahon visited the Battalion, and asked after the men of the Rangers. He expressed to the Commanding Officer his deep sympathy with the Battalion in its heavy losses, and remarked that he always tried to give the Rangers a good show, but he thought they always got the hard knocks.   He was very pleased with what they had done.

A post of 30 men was sent down to the bottom of the pass to reinforce the Cyclists in the evening. The mist never cleared off all day, and at times completely obscured the whole countryside.

Orders were received for the Rangers to rejoin the 30th Brigade after they were relieved from the duty in Dedeli pass.

Soon after midnight orders were received to march at once to Scott's Corner and there rejoin the 30th Brigade.   This was received at 12.25 a.m. on 11th December, and although it was almost impossible to see even a foot away, so thick was the mist and so dark the night, the Battalion was on the march to Scott's Corner at 1.25 a.m., which was reached at 2.10 a.m.   The Battalion was then halted until 4.5 a.m., as the 6th and 7th Royal Munster Fusiliers had not arrived.

When the Brigade began the march to Dojran, the 7th Royal Dublin Fusiliers led, and the 5th Battalion the Connaught Rangers, 6th Royal Dublin Fusiliers, 6th and 7th Royal Munster Fusiliers, and 10th Hampshire Regiment in the order mentioned. The Brigade halted for ten minutes every hour.

At 6.15 a.m. three heavy reports sounded behind the column, in the direction of Dedeli, evidently the bridges being destroyed in the pass.

At 7.10 a.m. on the 11th December the Brigade reached the outskirts of Dojran, and passed a French Mountain Battery proceeding in the direction of Dedeli.

On arrival at Dojran the 5th Connaught Rangers and 10th Hampshires were ordered by Brig.-General Vandeleur to continue their march to the Aviation Ground near the station, which was reached at 8.50 a.m. The 30th Brigade halted before arrival at Dojran station, and moved on to Kilindir later in the day.

The Battalion now rejoined the 29th Brigade. The early morning had been wet, foggy, and the weather was very cold ; the roads were thick with mud which made marching heavy for all. On the march to Dojran the Battalion passed the 65th Brigade, which had been brought up from Salonika, and which were fitted with leather jerkins and sheepskin coats, towards which the men who had been serving on the Bulgarian frontier, with no more than a great-coat, cast longing eyes.

At 12.30 p.m. the sound of gun and rifle fire was heard across the lake Dojran, which proved that part of the then rearguard was engaged with the enemy.

The Greek frontier was crossed before the arrival at the Aviation Ground, where the Battalion had breakfast, and then moved a few hundred yards over to where the Headquarters of the Brigade was situated.   As the Battalion marched through the town of Dojran, down which large numbers of French soldiers had been marching towards the railway, the Serbian women and girls who had been living in the town began to evacuate their houses and to march with immense loads on their backs towards the Greek frontier.   Women, girls, and old men, weighed down by their worldly belongings, tramped along the muddy road, sobbing bitterly.   It was a heartrending sight and drew compassion from the soldiers, who had themselves lately gone through great trials.   The Battalion had marched ten miles to Dojran.   The railway station at Dojran was quite blocked with troops and loaded wagons all destined for Salonika.

Late in the afternoon the 29th Brigade was ordered to be ready to move at short notice. Officers and men lay down to try and get a short rest on the hard and cold ground, but at 12.30 orders were received to be ready to move at once.   The battalions fell in within a few minutes, and then came orders to fall out for a short time, while commanding officers were called to the Brigade Headquarters, when instructions were given out that the Brigade would have to fall in later on a given signal.

At 2.20 a.m. on the 12th December the Brigade was assembled again in the foggy, damp, and chilly morning.   The regiments marched off in fours, but after some way were halted and closed up. After a short wait the different battalions were led off again, and after marching for some miles across unknown and very broken country, the Brigade was again halted and closed up.

The Commanding Officers were told that the Brigade was going to act as rearguard and was to take up a certain position before dawn. At a few minutes to 6 a.m. the Rangers found themselves on the top of a hill near the frontier line, where the men were required to extend and hold a line just behind the frontier between Greece and Serbia. Although the men had no entrenching implements except their short service tools, very good work was soon done.

The 10th Hampshires and the Rangers were put on 12th December into the front line, and the 6th Leinsters were at first put into Serbian territory, but later were withdrawn behind the border line. The morning was not only misty, but there was a thin drizzle falling. The weather was cold, and before the Battalion came to a standstill, all the men were quite wet through. When the mist slightly lifted the line was rectified as far as possible, but it was quite impossible to even see the exact position of the different regiments. The tall lank grass covered with mist and light rain saturated the clothing of all ranks, who had only in a few cases the protection even of a greatcoat. The Brigadier went away for some hours, and left Lieut.-Colonel Jourdain in temporary command of the Brigade.

At 2 p.m. orders were received for the regiments of the Brigade to retire, directly on receipt of instructions from the French General, Leblois,

who was in charge of all the troops covering the
retirement.

At 5 p.m. word came that the French were
beginning to retire, and at 5.14 p.m. some regiments began to retire through the line. A little
firing broke out in front, but this soon subsided.
The Brigade sat down to wait for the signal,
but no signal came, and they accordingly spent
the night on the bleak hill-side.

The men had been over twelve nights by this
time on outpost duty without almost a break, and
duty became exceedingly heavy especially in the
Battalion and in the 10th Hampshires. Both
officers and men had no covering by day or night,
and the majority of the Battalion had only their
serge clothing, which had been often wet through
for days together. It was now ascertained that
a Battalion of French infantry was actually entrenched in the immediate front of the left of the
Brigade, but had been obscured by the thick mist
that overhung the country.

There were several French regiments well entrenched, among which the 235th Reserve Regiment of the line was near the Rangers.

The Brigade waited in the thick mist for the
order to move throughout the night, but no
further instructions were received. The fog
saturated every one, and the night was besides
very cold and wet.

Early on the morning of the 13th December it
was found necessary to send back to the few
limbers parked some distance behind the line for
rations, but these did not arrive until 8 a.m.,

when they were at once served out to the men. The mist and fog cleared up later, and it was then easy to see how part of the line had been extended in front of the remainder, and this alone might have caused a catastrophe.

The Rangers on the left and the Leinsters on the right took over the front line, and the 10th Hampshires and the 6th Royal Irish Rifles were in reserve. The line was laid out by the Brigadier, and Lieut.-Colonel Jourdain was put in command of the line. The Brigadier retained command of the second line.

The men were truly in a deplorable state, having had no change of any kind since the middle of November, and many had boots worn out, trousers worn out, and lying wet through day and night on the damp and muddy ground. The officers were in a pitiable state, but no murmur or complaint was ever heard. Ammunition was scarce, and some men had less than five rounds. What was worse, none could be got, and although every endeavour was made by the regimental authorities to obtain clothing and ammunition, this could not be done.

A patrol of the 6th Leinsters proceeding beyond the frontier line was taken by the Bulgarians. Lieut. Tibbs was sent down sick on 13th December, and there were now only 5 officers for Battalion duty.

Large numbers of the enemy were seen just before dusk moving into Dojran with artillery, proceeding from Dolozeli. This was at 3.40 p.m., and the force was estimated at a Division with artillery.

The Commanding Officer requested that the

Battalion should be released from outpost duty, as already this had been continuous since the 29th November. The Royal Irish Rifles were accordingly brought up in relief on the 14th December. The outpost line was now situated only a few yards behind the frontier line between Greece and Serbia.

Small parties of the enemy were observed on the hills behind Dojran and about a mile from the Rangers' position, but the road to Dojran was patrolled and picqueted by the Bulgarians within sight of our lines.

It was an extraordinary position, and the disposition of extending a thin line a few yards behind the boundary was provocative in the extreme. The French officers of the 235th Regiment, which was stationed next to the Rangers, were of the same opinion.

The night, however, passed without incident, and at 8 a.m. on the 14th December the Royal Irish Rifles began to take over the front line, as the Rangers were promised a rest. The Battalion took up a position in the second line during the morning. In the afternoon at 1.40 p.m. Brig.-General Vandeleur informed the Commanding Officer that it was probable that the Brigade would move the same night. Nothing was known then for certain, but all units were to be prepared to move.

The 10th Hampshires would move off in the first place, and would be followed by the Rangers, then the Leinsters, and finally the Royal Irish Rifles.

The weather now became piercing cold, and a chilling wind blew over the hill-tops, and the troops felt the cold severely. Orders for the prospective move were received at 7.35 p.m., and then came a long and tiring wait in the cold driving wind.

About 11.50 p.m. orders for the march, when ordered, were received.

At 2 a.m. on the 15th December, orders to move at 4 a.m. were received. The companies were ordered to move in at 3 a.m. and to be ready to march off at 3.45 a.m., as the Battalion was to be at the point of assembly at 4.30 a.m. The difficulties proved almost insuperable, but every one worked splendidly to play the game.

The moon had gone down at 2 a.m., and at 4 a.m. it was pitch dark. It was impossible to see even a yard in front.

The companies of the Battalion, however, left their positions, extended over a large tract of country, and made their way to the Battalion assembly post, and thereafter to the Brigade position on the road to Kilindir through an almost unmarked small track and interminable bushes to the road and after that to the Ford, about two miles on a very dark night too. The assembly post was not reached until 5.45 a.m., over an hour late, but the other two regiments of the Brigade were later still, as they had a longer march than the Rangers. The night had at first been cold but fine, but afterwards a drizzling rain began to fall, and later this became quite heavy.

The column arrived at Kilindir station a little after 8 a.m., and the Rangers and 10th Hampshires were ordered to remain and get a train to Salonika. The other two regiments continued the march with the Brigade transport by the road, which ran almost parallel to the railway. The march to Kilindir was eight miles long. Here the station was crowded with French soldiers and their baggage and transport.

Some few miles away the Bulgarian army must have viewed the retirement of the force, almost within striking distance, but the 29th Brigade was never molested.

The rain, which had begun about 4.30 a.m., continued all through the day, and when at 1.30 p.m. a troop train of vans was placed at the disposal of the two regiments, 10th Hampshires and the Rangers, the men were only too eager to get some cover from the inclemency of the weather. However, no engine was available until 7.10 p.m., when the tired and sleepy soldiers, after having submitted to endless shunting and moving backwards and forwards, saw the train leave Kilindir for Salonika.

Several stops occurred, but at 7.5 a.m. on the 16th December this train arrived at the Military Siding at Salonika. During the wait at Kilindir, battalions, batteries, and Chasseurs d'Afrique continually passed the station, moving south in an endless stream; while the same cheerful demeanour was apparent everywhere on all the French troops.

Soon after arrival at Salonika, tea and biscuits

were served out to all ranks, and were very much appreciated by the officers and men of the Battalion.

After breakfast the Battalion marched about a mile northwards up the road to the camp of the 22nd Division, where the officers and men were accommodated in tents. Rain, however, soon began to fall, and drenched the unfortunate men, who had barely got dry from the previous day's downpour.

The 30th Brigade was at this time moving from camp near by to Kapajilar, on the southeast of Salonika.

At 9 a.m. the Rangers marched up the muddy road to the camp, which was reached a little before 10 a.m. A Serbian Regiment passed the camp at 10.20 a.m., moving northwards. The men were particularly fine and well set up. They were re-equipped with the French rifle and ammunition.

The whole camp soon became quite a sea of mud and water, and everything seemed saturated with the heavy downpour of rain. Tents, a luxury the Battalion had not enjoyed for over a month, were, however, a great consolation. Brig.-General Nicol visited the Battalion on his way to Kapajilar, and requested Lieut.-Colonel Jourdain to apportion the camps to the other brigades and regiments of the Division.

The men were allowed to remain in their tents till 7.30 a.m. on the 17th December, and then all numbers were checked with the Battalion books, as this could not be done before.

The Headquarters of the 29th Brigade and the

Leinster Regiment arrived by train at Salonika at 11.20 p.m. on the same date (17th December).

New clothing was at once obtained for the men, and boots and other articles of equipment were indented for, to replace those worn out or lost.

On the 18th December a draft of 90 men arrived to join the Battalion, chiefly details from the Base Depôt. The Irish Rifles had joined the Brigade early on this date.

The War Office telegram of the 14th December, 1915, is given here :—

'The Anglo-French Corps continue to make an orderly retreat in Macedonia. The retirement of the British forces from Lake Dojran to a position further west was greatly helped by the gallantry of the 10th Division, which included several Irish regiments. Eight guns had to be abandoned, and our casualties amounted to 1,500 men. The enemy bulletins give highly-coloured accounts of the Bulgarian pursuit and of the demoralization of the Entente forces. The Athenian newspaper in touch with German circles report that, out of consideration to Greek susceptibilities, Bulgarian troops will not cross the frontier in pursuit of the Allies, and that their place alongside of the Germanic armies will be taken by three Turkish Divisions.'

On the 19th December the work of re-equipping the Battalion went rapidly on, and orders were received to be ready for a move within about three days. This, however, never occurred.

Two drafts composed of N.C.O.s and men of

o

the Connaught Rangers, which had been attached to the Inniskilling Fusiliers and the Royal Irish Fusiliers, rejoined the Battalion this day, as the men did not wish to remain with those regiments, and the Brigadier-General commanding the 31st Brigade had consented to allow these men to join their own Regiment. There were 5 officers and 375 other ranks in all, most of whom had taken part in some of the actions in Serbia on the 7th and 8th December.

The officers were :—

2nd Lieut. J. A. Calderwood, 4th Scottish Rifles.

2nd Lieut. H. McCulloch, 11th Royal Scots.

2nd Lieut. J. J. Pope, 14th Royal Scots.

2nd Lieut. A. M. Lumsden, 4th Argyll and Sutherland Highlanders.

2nd Lieut. J. C. McIntosh, 13th Highland Light Infantry, and

2nd Lieut. C. E. Gallwey, who also returned from hospital the same day.

All the men were Connaught Rangers from 3rd or 4th Battalions.

The total strength of the Battalion was now 17 officers and 1,046 other ranks.

The Brigade was ordered to move in a few days to the Gulf of Rendina to take up the line between the Lake Beshik and the sea (Gulf of Rendina or Orfano).

The Battalion transport rejoined the Regiment on 19th December, having marched from Kilindir by a track close to the railway. Several carts were, however, smashed by the rough road by which they had to travel.

On the 20th December the work of re-equipping 1915 the 375 men who had returned from the 31st Brigade was pressed on.   Sheepskins and leather jerkins were now given out to the men for the first time, and nothing was spared to make the men comfortable and warm in the winter weather that had already broken.

On the 21st December 29 men arrived from the Base Depôt, still further increasing the strength of the Battalion.

The 31st Brigade marched away to its allotted position east of Salonika on the 22nd December. The name of Brig.-General J. R. Longley, East Surrey Regiment, was in orders this day as having assumed command of the Division in place of Lieut.-General Sir B. T. Mahon.

Both Serbian and French regiments passed the camp of the Battalion the same day, proceeding up to the French lines, and on the 23rd December large French reinforcements arrived. The work of equipping the new arrivals was still in process of completion on the 23rd December, when orders were received that the Brigade would probably remain at Salonika over Christmas.

Many of the young officers, who had borne with patience and great courage their exposure and privations on the Bulgarian and Greek frontiers, now showed signs of the hardships they had undergone, but none had given in and reported sick.

It can now be stated that the great strain incurred by all, and especially by those in authority, of those long drawn-out days on the Greek frontier, when the men were practically unarmed, following on the nerve-racking days on the ridge above Kosturino, had been very great. When, however, the train had left Kilindir, it was felt that the atmosphere had cleared, and although one train had been wrecked only a few days before between that station and Salonika, officers and men alike lay down on floors of the bare and dirty vans in which they were collected and slept soundly.

The change to inaction at Salonika was most refreshing, and the possession of even a tent made the past seem quite remote.

On the 24th December Brig.-General Longley came up and interviewed the Battalion commanders at 1.30 p.m.

Christmas Day at Salonika broke with the whole country white with frost, and the hills around were covered with snow. There was parade for the troops for divine service, and the drums of the Battalion played before and after service. A ration of beer was obtained for the men through the exertions of some officers, and in the evening the drums played patriotic airs which were much appreciated by all and also by the 6th Leinster Regiment, which was encamped alongside the Rangers.

This day the following Order was received :—

' 10th Irish Division.

' Special Order.

' Lieut.-General Sir B. T. Mahon, on relinquishing the command of the 10th Irish Division, which he had the honour of raising and com-

manding until he received command of the
Salonika Army, desires to express his thanks for
the loyal and faithful support he has received
from all ranks, during the hard work and severe
strain caused by heavy casualties on active service, whilst serving on the Peninsula and in
Serbia. He wishes the Division good luck in
the future, and feels convinced that all members
of it, knowing how highly their work in the past
has been appreciated by His Majesty, will redouble
their efforts to maintain the noble traditions of
their regiments and corps, and by good discipline
and cheerily meeting and overcoming all difficulties, help to bring the war to a successful and
early end.

'(Sd.) D. SAPTE, Colonel.

'A.A. and Q.M.G., 10th Irish Division.

'23 Dec., 1915.'

The following is an extract from the 10th Irish
Division Orders dated 23rd December, 1915 :—

No. 91.

Message from the King.

The Army Commander has received a gracious
telegraphic message from His Majesty the King,
in which His Majesty expressed his appreciation of
the manner in which the 10th Division carried out
the operations entrusted to them in Serbia. His
Majesty also graciously inquires after the welfare
of the sick and wounded. To the Royal message
of appreciation, the Army Commander has replied
as follows :—

' The King—Buckingham Palace, London.

' All ranks 10th Division respectfully thank His Majesty for his gracious message, which will stimulate them to renewed exertions. Sick and wounded doing well.

' General Mahon.'

The Church services which had been arranged for Sunday, 26th December, were cancelled by order of the Brigadier, and the Brigade was ordered to be ready to move shortly.

The following special Army Order was received :

25th Dec. 1915.

The following gracious message from His Majesty the King has just been received by the Army Commander :—

' Another Christmas finds all the resources of the Empire still engaged in war, and we desire to convey on our behalf and on behalf of the Queen a heartfelt Christmas greeting and our good wishes for the New Year to all who on sea and land are upholding the honour of the British name.   In the officers and men of my Navy on whom the security of the Empire depends, I repose in common with all my subjects a trust that is absolute.   On the officers and men of my Army, whether now in France, in the East or in other fields, I rely with an equal faith, confident that their devotion, their valour, and their self-sacrifice will under God's guidance lead to victory and an honourable peace. There are many of their comrades now, alas, in hospital, and to those brave men also I desire with

the Queen to express our deep gratitude and our
earnest prayers for their recovery.

Officers and men of the Navy and of the Army,
another year is drawing to a close, as it began, in
toil, bloodshed, and suffering, but I rejoice to know
the goal which you are striving for draws nearer
into sight ; and may God bless you and all your
undertakings.'

(Sd.) Travers Clarke, Brig.-General.

Deputy Adjutant and Q.M.-General.

These kind messages were all read to the troops.
To the regret of all ranks Captain G. J. B. E. Massy,
whose arm had never recovered from the wound
received by him on 10th August, was admitted to
hospital on the 26th December, and with Lieut.
Tibbs was later invalided to England. Captain
Massy had acted as Adjutant of the Battalion
since the 25th September, including the move to
Salonika, and the operations in Serbia and on the
Bulgarian frontier, and by his unfailing tact and
devotion to duty had done so much to make the
Battalion what it was.

Captain R. R. Martin took over the duties of
Adjutant as a temporary measure. All heavy kit
was sent down to the Harbour on the 27th December to be loaded for Rendina.

Lieut. and Temp.-Captain D. P. J. Kelly was
admitted to hospital the same evening. There
were now only the following officers who had proceeded with the Battalion to Serbia in November :

Lieut.-Colonel Jourdain (Commanding).

2nd Lieut. H. J. Shanley.

2nd Lieut. F. W. Illingworth (Scottish Rifles, attached).

2nd Lieut. H. C. Bell (Signal Officer, attached).

2nd Lieut. G. F. Macnie (Transport Officer, attached).

Lieut. O'Sullivan, R.A.M.C.

Lieut. and Quartermaster Farrell.

Seven officers had been killed, wounded, or were missing, and seven officers had been invalided through sickness. The only two officers who had done Company duty for the period were 2nd Lieuts. Shanley and Illingworth.

Captain Martin and Lieut. Fogarty had joined the Battalion in Serbia or Bulgaria.

The Battalion commenced to march into Salonika at 5.35 a.m. on the 28th December, to embark for Rendina Bay. After an uneventful march of over four and a half miles, the Rangers reached the English Quay at 7.42 a.m., and began to embark on lighters almost at once. The Headquarters and the greater part of the Battalion left the quay at 8.40 a.m. and reached H.M. Transport   at 9.20 a.m. The Rangers and the 30th Field Ambulance were embarked on the   , and all troops were safely on board this vessel at 10 a.m. The day was beautifully fine and bright, and at 2.40 p.m. the transport commenced to move down the harbour, but later anchored for a short time near H.M.S. *Exmouth*.

At 3 p.m. the   steered out to sea, escorted by two destroyers. The transports were, besides the   , the   , the   , and   . These were ordered to proceed

in line ahead and at not more than ten knots an
hour.   The evening closed with a brilliant sunset,
and afterwards all lights were extinguished on board.

The convoy arrived in Rendina Bay at 7.46 a.m.
on the 29th December, and the different transports
anchored at once.   Troops were warned to be
ready to disembark without delay.

At 10 a.m., however, two lighters came alongside
the   , and at 10.17 a.m. the first lighter
left for the shore, and all men were disembarked
from the first lighter at 11 a.m., the naval
authorities making a bridge of boats from the
lighters to the shore.   By midday the whole of the
Battalion, except the fatigue party left on board,
was disembarked and bivouacked on shore.   The
work of unloading the heavy kit of the Battalion
was expeditiously and exceedingly well carried out,
and the whole was completed by 6.30 p.m., when
all the Battalion's blankets, stores, bivouacs, tents
and ammunition, as well as the Brigade ammunition reserve, had been brought ashore and stacked
or distributed.

The Naval Transport Officer cordially congratulated the Battalion on their splendid work.
The Rangers were the first to complete their disembarkation.

The Bay was situated at the mouth of the
Rendina river, the outlet of Lake Beshik, and was
surrounded by hills, which were covered with a low
holly scrub.

The village of Skala Stavros was near the
bivouac of the Brigade.

After the sun set, fires were lighted on the beach

in order to carry on the work of disembarkation, which went on throughout the night.

A thick white frost covered the whole country-side on the morning of the 30th December, and the work of bringing on shore the stores went on without intermission.

The effective strength of the Battalion on this day was as follows :—

15 officers.
1,038 other ranks.
11 riding horses.
43 draught mules.
8 pack mules.
16 limber wagons.
4 machine-guns.

The transport rejoined the Battalion the same day, having marched from Salonika by Lakes Langaza and Beshik.

Supplies for fifteen days had been brought with the force.

At 8 a.m. on the 31st December the Commanding Officers of the Brigade were required to meet the Brigadier, and to ride round the position to be held by the Brigade. Under the scheme the Connaught Rangers would hold the right of the line towards the sea at Rendina Bay.

At 1 p.m. the Battalion paraded and marched over to the new position, which was reached at 2.30 p.m. Here the Rangers bivouacked and made ready to spend the last night of the departing year.

Captain Shaw, who had left the Battalion in

August to assume the duties of Staff-Captain of the Brigade, was admitted to hospital and left for England in January. The weather, which had hitherto been fine at Rendina, broke the same evening and heavy rain fell throughout the night.

The morning of the 1st January 1916 broke with heavy rain still falling, and this continued until 3 p.m. The men had had, however, just sufficient time on the previous night to put up their bivouacs, and were consequently saved some discomfort. Captain Martin, who had officiated as Adjutant of the Battalion since Captain Massy left, was ordered to vacate the appointment by the Brigadier, and Captain C. J. Lyster, of the 6th Leinster Regiment, arrived and took over the Adjutancy by order of the Brigadier.

On the 2nd January the work of cutting paths up the steep wooded sides of the range of hills on which trenches were to be dug was carried on with excellent results. Miles of pathway were cut and rendered fit for mules or riding horses, and considering that the number of cutting tools was so limited, the amount of work completed was extraordinary. The men of the Battalion worked so very well at this work.

On the 3rd January Surgeon-General W. G. Macpherson, C.B., C.M.G., visited the bivouac of the Rangers and expressed his great approval of the cleanliness, order, and condition of the men and the camp.

B and C Companies were sent up to occupy the bivouac on the top of the hill overlooking Vrasta on the afternoon of the 3rd January.

These companies

were ordered to dig certain trenches in accordance with instructions received from the Brigadier.

On the 4th January one Company of the 6th Leinster Regiment was moved up near the Rangers, and every available man was at work on making roads and communication paths between all the posts on top of the range. This fatigue lasted all day long, and was very well done by all the men.

At 2.15 p.m. the Brigadier visited the companies at work and expressed his approbation of the work done.

Fatigue on communication roads and cutting down brushwood went on all day on the 5th January. An inspection of work done and trenches to be dug was commenced by the Brigadier at 9 a.m. on the 6th January, but was not completed until 1.20 p.m. The Officer Commanding the Brigade personally pointed out every site for every trench, but these were not allowed to be taken in hand as yet. The day was very cold and sunless, and at 6.20 p.m. rain began to fall heavily.

The enemy's aeroplanes began to visit the line almost daily and to see what work was being carried on along the Rendina Boghazi. On the 7th January two of these visited the Rendina position.

Captain W. W. MacNaught, R.A.M.C., joined the Battalion in place of Captain J. I. O'Sullivan, R.A.M.C., as Medical Officer, who joined the 30th Field Ambulance. It was with feelings of regret that all ranks of the 5th Battalion said farewell to Captain O'Sullivan, who had been with the Battalion throughout the campaigns in Gallipoli and Serbia, displaying the greatest devotion to duty and always willing to help those who sought his aid. His name was submitted for consideration.

There were now only two officers who had been with the Battalion throughout the campaign —Lieut.-Colonel Jourdain (in command), and Lieut. Farrell (the Quartermaster).

On the 8th January the Brigadier again went round the line and changed several of the sites for trenches, which had been already dug. The men accordingly began to dig new trenches and machine-gun positions.

Another German aeroplane flew over the bivouac on the 8th January.

The island of Thasos could be seen from the spur above the camp, and the sea-coast almost to Kavalla was clearly perceptible.

The lines were again inspected by the Brigadier on the 9th January. All men that could be spared from fatigue attended service, celebrated by the chaplains near the Headquarters bivouac.

On the 10th January Lieut.-Colonel Jourdain was sent to the 30th Field Ambulance sick, and on his way down to the Field Ambulance was accompanied by all the officers then with the Battalion. Lieut.-Colonel Jourdain had commanded the Regiment from the 19th August, 1914, the date of its formation, up to this date, and had not been absent from duty the whole period the Battalion had been abroad.

1916   The Rev. T. J. O'Connor, Roman Catholic Chaplain to the Forces, who had made his home with the Connaught Rangers since the move from Anzac and who had been all through the campaign with the 29th Brigade, was present with the Battalion on this day. His services to the Battalion had been beyond all praise, and his work for men of the Regiment had been most heavy, and his name was submitted to higher authority for devotion to duty and good service.

Captain C. J. J. Lyster assumed command of the Battalion on Lieut.-Colonel Jourdain's admission to hospital.

On the 10th January the Battalion was ordered to move at some near date to the west end of the Rendina gorge. Temp.-Major V. M. Scully was then ordered by the Brigadier to assume command of the Battalion from Major 10th Hampshire Regiment.

The following letters were received by the Commanding Officer from retired officers of the Rangers, and are here given :—

FROM MAJOR-GENERAL W. L. DALRYMPLE, C.B.,
COLONEL OF THE CONNAUGHT RANGERS.

Inverarm,
Camberley, Surrey,
20 Nov., 1915.

DEAR JOURDAIN,

It was good of you sending me the account of your Battalion's doings. It was most interesting, and I should love to hear any further accounts

that you may find it possible to send me. I read 1916
it to the 6th Battalion and showed it to Owen,
F. Hutchinson, and Owen agrees with me that
it should be published in the Irish papers. Will
you give me permission to do it, merely suppress-
ing your name? I think it is due to the Regiment
that their noble deeds should be made public,
and it should help recruiting for the Rangers
generally. Please take an early opportunity of
expressing to the Battalion my great pride as
Colonel of the Regiment in reading of their
splendid behaviour and dash in action. They
have added laurels to the many gathered during
the last 100 years and more by the Rangers, and
I would not change my Colonelcy of the Regiment
for that of any other in His Majesty's service.
Give me the permission I ask for, that Ireland may
be as proud of the Rangers as I am.

Good luck to you and the Battalion.

Ever yours sincerely,

(Sd.) W. L. DALRYMPLE.

Colonel A. A. Owen, M.V.O., writes as follows :—

Polesdon,

Datchet,

Friday, Nov. 19, 1915.

DEAR JOURDAIN,

Dalrymple sent me this morning your excellent
description of the gallant services of the 5th
Battalion of the Rangers. A record they will
ever be proud of, reflecting all honour to our
regimental history. May I be allowed to convey

1916 through you to all ranks, officers and men, my heartfelt congratulations and expressions of the belief that they will always support their fighting reputation when called on to face the music. Although a worn-out old Ranger of 74 years of age, my memory of some 25 years in the Regiment will never be forgotten as the happiest of my life. I wish I was young enough to be with you now.

With every hearty wish to you all,

Yours ever,

(Sd.) ARTHUR ALLEN OWEN.

The third letter, from Colonel C. E. Wyncoll, late of the Connaught Rangers and A.S.C., was as under :—

Headquarters, Eastern Command,

Horse Guards,

London, S.W.

13 Dec., 1915.

MY DEAR JOURDAIN,

Accept my great admiration and sincere congratulation to yourself and the 5th Battalion of the old Regiment that you command, for the glorious work you did on the 11th and the splendid way you upheld the traditions with the cold steel. I would rather have had the honour to do what you have done than be made K.G. Let some one else write the account in the regimental history. More power.

Yours always,

(Sd.) C. E. WYNCOLL.

These letters were duly promulgated to all
ranks before the departure of the Battalion from
Salonika on Christmas Eve.   Several other letters
from retired officers of the Regiment were received, congratulating the Battalion on its service
in Gallipoli and Serbia.

B and D Companies moved up to the west end
of the gorge on the 11th January.

On the 13th January a Taube which had just
flown over the lines, suddenly began to drop,
and a loud explosion occurred.   The machine was
seen to make seawards, but after flying a short
distance, it fell and plunged into the sea.   The
observer threw himself out, but the machine and
both occupants fell into the sea and sank.   A
look-out was kept for the observer on the machine,
but nothing was seen of either afterwards.

A severe frost covered the whole countryside
on the 14th January with its snow-white cloak.

A third Company of the Battalion moved up
the gorge to the west end in pouring rain which
continued throughout the night.   On the 15th
snow began to fall, and the hills soon became
covered with white.

Major B. R. Cooper rejoined the Battalion on
the 16th January with 88 men.

On the 17th January Lieut.-Colonel Jourdain
requested the Officer Commanding to publish the
following farewell order :—

' After having raised the Fifth Battalion of the
Rangers, and having had the honour to command
it continuously ever since, Lieut.-Colonel Jourdain
bids farewell to the Battalion with keen sorrow

P

1916 and sincere regret. He heartily thanks all those who have loyally worked for the good of the Regiment, and who have assisted him in the undertakings he has been called on to perform. He will ever remember those gallant spirits who, answering to the country's call, and who now rest in a soldier's grave in the Peninsula and in Serbia, did so much to bring fame to Ireland and immortal glory to the Regiment to which they belonged.

' To those officers, warrant officers, non-commissioned officers and men, who have borne the stress of two campaigns, and to those who have joined the Battalion from other Corps or from other Battalions of the Rangers, and who have fought for and made their home in the Fifth Rangers, he tenders his grateful thanks for work well and loyally done, and his sincere admiration for the many gallant deeds which have made the name of the 5th Battalion of the Rangers known throughout the Army, and which have wrung unstinted praise from all those who have known the Battalion in Anzac or in Serbia.'

In Sir Ian Hamilton's dispatch dated 11th December 1915, and published in the papers of 29th January 1916, the following officers, warrant and non-commissioned officers and men, are brought to notice :—

CONNAUGHT RANGERS (SERVICE BATTALION).

Major (Temp. Lieut.-Colonel) H. F. N. Jourdain, Connaught Rangers.

Temp.-Major N. C. K. Money (Captain 22nd Punjabis).

Temp.-Major B. R. Cooper.

Captain G. J. B. E. Massy (Connaught Rangers).

Captain H. B. W. Maling (Connaught Rangers), Adjutant.

Temp.-Lieut. A. J. W. Blake (killed).

Lieut. S. H. Lewis (Connaught Rangers).

No. 3,010, Temp. Sergt.-Major J. Hudson.

No. 5/319, Sergt. (Acting Company Q.M.-Sergt.) M. Nealon.

No. 5/642, Sergeant J. O'Connell.

No. 6,757, Sergeant J. McIlwain.

No. 5/824, Private (Acting Corporal) J. Doyle.

No. 5/83, Private J. Geehan.

No. 5/3831, Private J. Sweeney.

No. 529, Private M. Kilroy.

The following Honours were conferred in a Supplement to the *London Gazette* dated 2nd February, 1916 :—

Order of St. Michael and St. George. To be C.M.G.

Major (Temp. Lieut.-Colonel) Henry F. N. Jourdain, the Connaught Rangers.

To be a Companion of the Distinguished Service Order.

Captain (Temp.-Major) Noel Campbell Kyrle Money, 22nd Punjabis, Indian Army, attached Connaught Rangers (Service Battalion).

To receive the Military Cross.

Captain Godfrey J. B. E. Massy, Connaught Rangers (attached Service Battalion).

To receive the Distinguished Conduct Medal.

5/83, Private J. Geehan, 5th Battalion the Connaught Rangers.

5/642, Sergeant J. O'Connell, 5th Battalion the Connaught Rangers.

Clasp to Distinguished Conduct Medal.

No. 5/3010, Sergeant-Major J. Hudson, 5th Battalion Connaught Rangers.

The Distinguished Conduct Medal was awarded for services in the South African War, 1901–2, whilst belonging to the Irish Guards.

In the recipients of Honours conferred in the *London Gazette* of the 3rd June 1916, Temp. 2nd Lieut. G. Robinson, 5th (Service) Battalion the Connaught Rangers, received the Military Cross for the operations in Serbia in November and December 1915, and No. 5,582, Pte. J. Folan, the D.C.M.

In Sir Ian Hamilton's dispatch of December 11th, 1915, which was published in the papers of 7th January, 1916, it was stated that :—

' The advance of the left section was a success ; after a brisk engagement the Well at Kabak Kuyu was seized by the Indian Brigade,' &c.

To rectify this mistake Lieut.-Colonel Jourdain wrote to Lieut.-General Sir A. J. Godley, K.C.M.G., C.B., and asked him to try and get the mistake put right, and the capture of the Wells attributed to the Rangers.

Lieut.-General Sir Alexander Godley at once sent the following letter to Lieut.-Colonel Jourdain, and enclosed a copy of the communication he had also sent to the Military Secretary, M.E.F., in order to have the necessary correction made. The letters are as follows :—

Headquarters,

2nd Australian and New Zealand Army Corps,

Ismailia, 20*th April*, 1916.

MY DEAR JOURDAIN,

I am very glad you wrote to me about the taking of Kaiajik Aghala. I had noticed it myself, but as later on your Battalion was so favourably mentioned, I had not thought it necessary to draw attention to the obvious mistake, but you are perfectly right, and I enclose copy of a letter which I have written on the subject, which may lead to the necessary alteration being made.

I thank you very much for your very kind congratulations. In return I am very glad to be able to congratulate you. I shall be proud if I have a Battalion of your Regiment serving under me again.

Yours very sincerely,

(Sd.) ALEX. GODLEY.

Lieut.-Colonel H. F. N. Jourdain, C.M.G.

The Connaught Rangers.

Headquarters,

2nd Australian and New Zealand Army Corps,

Ismailia, *20th April*, 1916.

Memorandum for

The Military Secretary,

Mediterranean Expeditionary Force.

I enclose herewith a letter from Lieut.-Colonel Jourdain, who commanded the 5th Battalion Connaught Rangers at the attack on the Kaiajik Aghala in August last. His contention is correct, and I should be glad if the necessary correction may be made. If, in the last two lines of page 44 of the Dispatch as published in pamphlet form, the words 'Connaught Rangers' were substituted for 'Indian Brigade', the matter would be put right.

(Sd.) ALEX. GODLEY, Lieut.-General.

Late Commanding New Zealand and Australian Division.

Sec. Lieut. (Temp. Lieut.) D. P. J. Kelly was awarded the Military Cross on August 21, 1916, for gallantry during the operations in Serbia in December 1915.

CASUALTIES IN 5TH BATTALION THE CONNAUGHT RANGERS.

FROM JULY 1915—DECEMBER 1915.

	Officers killed or died of wounds.	Officers wounded.	Officers missing.	Officers sick.	Other ranks killed.	Other ranks wounded.	Other ranks missing.	Other ranks sick.	Total all ranks.
Lone Pine trenches, Chunak Bair, and up to 20th August.	1	5 (3 wounded twice)	—	1	15	120	—	78	220
Capture of Kabak Kuyu Wells, on 21st August.	3	9	—	—	43	159	47	7	268
Capture of Hill 60, Kaiajik Aghala, and losses between 22nd and 27th.	—	1	1 missing and wounded, believed killed.	—	(killed and wounded) 152	3	—	not known	157
S.W.B. Gully and Bauchop's Hill and up to end of Sept.	1	—	—	2	4	32	—	not known	39
Operations in Serbia and on Bulgarian Frontier and in Greece.	4	3 (1 wounded and prisoner)	—	4	31	120	wounded and missing 38 missing 179	144	523
Other causes up to January 1916.	—	—	—	5	1	6	—	not known	12
Total.	9	18	1	12	94	440 plus 152	264	229 as far as known	1219

www.ingramcontent.com/pod-product-compliance
Lightning Source LLC
Chambersburg PA
CBHW070944150426
42812CB00066B/3274/J